A Psychoanalytic Perspective on Tragedy, Theater and Death

T0316336

A Psychoanalytic Perspective on Tragedy, Theater and Death shines a spotlight on what theater, and especially tragedy, tells us about our ontological selves by exploring both Euripides' *Bacchae* and the work of Tadeusz Kantor.

Focusing on the theatrical tradition of the West, the book examines Euripides' *Bacchae*, a tragedy about the nature of tragedy, suggesting that the tragic can be defined as an ontological duality rooted in the early experience of the infant's separation from mother, with whom s/he had, until then, formed a fused Unit. The traumatic rupture of this primal Unit is inscribed in the unconscious as death.

The book then considers the defining binary structure of the theatrical setting – (spectator/spectated or fantasy/reality) – before arguing that in staging our ontological dividedness, theater shows its relation to death to be organic. The book concludes by examining in detail the principal works of Polish theater director Tadeusz Kantor, whose search for theater's identity was, essentially, a search for human identity.

Erudite and far-reaching, *A Psychoanalytic Perspective on Tragedy, Theater and Death* will interest psychoanalysts as well as students, scholars and researchers across the dramatic arts wishing to draw on psychoanalytic ideas.

Konstantinos I. Arvanitakis is a Training and Supervising Analyst and former Director of the Canadian Institute of Psychoanalysis. He is an Associated Faculty member and Professor of Psychoanalysis and Philosophy at the Department of Philosophy, McGill University, and Emeritus Psychiatrist at the McGill University Health Center, Montreal, Canada.

A Psychoanalytic Perspective on Tragedy, Theater and Death

Tadeusz Kantor and the Ontology of the Self

Konstantinos I. Arvanitakis

Routledge
Taylor & Francis Group

LONDON AND NEW YORK

First published 2019
by Routledge
4 Park Square, Milton Park, Abingdon, Oxon OX14 4RN
605 Third Avenue, New York, NY 10017

First issued in paperback 2023

Routledge is an imprint of the Taylor & Francis Group, an informa business

British Library Cataloguing in Publication Data
A catalogue record for this book is available from the British Library

Library of Congress Cataloging in Publication Data
Names: Arvanitakis, Konstantinos I., author.
Title: A psychoanalytic perspective on tragedy, theatre and death :
    Tadeusz Kantor and the ontology of the self / Konstantinos I.
    Arvanitakis.
Description: Abingdon, Oxon ; New York, NY : Routledge, 2019. |
    Includes bibliographical references and index.
Identifiers: LCCN 2018052133 (print) | LCCN 2018055302 (ebook) |
    ISBN 9780429431470 (Master) | ISBN 9780429776083 (ePub) |
    ISBN 9780429776076 (Mobipocket) | ISBN 9780429776090 (Pdf) |
    ISBN 9781138364240 | ISBN 9781138364240
    (hardback : alk. paper) | ISBN 9780429431470 (ebk)
Subjects: LCSH: Kantor, Tadeusz, 1915–1990—Criticism and
    interpretation. | Tragedy—History and criticism. | Psychoanalysis
    and literature. | Self (Philosophy) in literature.
Classification: LCC PG7170.A54 (ebook) | LCC PG7170.A54 A78 2019
    (print) | DDC 809.2/512—dc23
LC record available at https://lccn.loc.gov/2018052133

ISBN: 978-1-03-257056-3 (pbk)
ISBN: 978-1-138-36424-0 (hbk)
ISBN: 978-0-429-43147-0 (ebk)

DOI: 10.4324/9780429431470

Typeset in Bembo
by Swales & Willis Ltd, Exeter, Devon, UK

Publisher's Note
The publisher has gone to great lengths to ensure the quality of this reprint but points
out that some imperfections in the original copies may be apparent.

A Mauro Bortoli
per le vocali . . .

Contents

Acknowledgments

I wish to gratefully acknowledge my debt to the staff of the Centre for the Documentation of the Art of Tadeusz Kantor for their gracious and generous assistance in providing Kantor's notebooks and other related documents.

Introduction

Two realities

If the world is a stage, the curtain of our eyelids condemns us to a double vision from which there is no escape. We are driven to construct "theories" (θεωρια means "view" of the images seen on either side of the eyelids, images that are frequently mutually exclusive and mutually obliterating much in the fashion of a figure-ground pattern. It would seem that the fundamental human task consists of an endless struggle to interrelate, to co-ordinate the scenes on the two stages on either side of a "curtain." We are, inescapably, diplopic spectators (θεαται) in a disarticulated double theater (θεατρον).

The psychoanalyst, a passionate spectator of an invisible Other, positions herself on the precarious threshold between the two "stages," sympathetically doubling herself in consonant correspondence with her interlocutor–analysand as both subject and object on either side of the curtain, thereby embodying the ontological human paradox.

We, in the West, being heirs of what has been called a "culture of the eyes,"[1] never ceased inquiring about the nature and origin of this radical dualism in our perception of reality. The enormous effort required to maintain a double vision, a "binocular" vision, leads to an irresistible proclivity to foreclose one of the two vistas with costly consequences. However, this is also what provides the motive for our continuous attempt to bring the two into a tolerant co-habitation, if not a creative intercourse.

An infant of four months is joyfully playing with a small toy, a furry little animal. At some point, the toy falls to the ground and disappears out of view. The infant shows no reaction to its disappearance and, as if nothing happened, quickly turns her attention to something else.

A slightly older infant is actively engaged with the little toy until an "evil" adult takes the toy and hides it behind a piece of cloth that happens to be in front of the child and is within her reach. The child begins to cry, showing her distress with agitated movements. It is she *herself* who seems to be at a loss, but she does nothing to retrieve the lost object. We may note here, among other things, the first definition of "evil" as a force coming from the outside world and being inseparably linked to loss.

A still older child, perhaps the same child as before – to whom we will now give a name, Theodora – is totally absorbed in her play with the little toy animal, until the irreverent hand takes it and hides it away. However, this time Theodora will promptly and confidently reach behind the cloth where she knows her cherished little animal *is* and, seizing it again, will continue her play.

The question of *being* has preoccupied *homo sapiens* ever since the dawn of consciousness. Being could be conceived only in relation to its absence: the concept of being arises as a function of its negation, at the moment of loss. A break in the continuity of "being-there" brings about what psychoanalysis considers a "catastrophic" moment, which calls forth urgent measures to ensure survival. Alkmaion of Croton formulated the human predicament quite early. In one of his surviving fragments, we read that

> *Humans perish because of their inability*
> *To join the end to the beginning.*[2]

In the course of individual cognitive development – which allows us to speculate that a similar evolution may have taken place in the development of the human species as well – the infant will develop the capacity to bestow continued existence to the absent object in a locus *other than the one given to the senses*. The lost object will be endowed with permanence, and later invested with constancy, thereby ensuring continuity in the service of life. Theodora's invisible object continues to exist – on the other side of the "curtain." It endures the transience and the coming-to-be and passing away of the perpetually changing world of the senses.

The human pain related to loss, the existential shock at the break of continuity, may explain, from a psychological vantage point, the drive of the early Greek philosophers at the infancy of Western thought to formulate and posit an enduring Principle (αρχη) that lies concealed behind the mutating world of appearances and guarantees its fundamental stability. Thus, we arrive at the earliest enunciation of a postulate of the existence of *two* realities – signifying a rupture in being – and of a principle of continuity that defies the schism.

It is this moment of abstraction, this leap of thought, accomplished by the Pre-Socratics that is the true "Greek Miracle," rather than the achievements of the Classical period to which this term usually refers and which can be considered as the direct expression of such a belief in an enduring Ideal. However, behind every "miracle" there is a "sentence," and the West has been condemned to the rending agonies of dualism ever since. The price for a reassuring sense of security is perpetual doubt. *Sum ergo dubito.*

The corollary of the postulate of an enduring substance behind the multiplicity of appearances is the belief in a meta-physical Unity that overrides the diversity of experience. The world is ordered (κοσμος) and held together by an underlying αρχη. This answers the primordial puzzle of the bewildering fragmentation of human experience but leaves forever open the question of how the One gave rise to the Many and how the Many can come together in the One. Empedokles:

> *A double tale shall I tell. At times One alone emerges from Many,*
> *At times, indeed, Many stem from One*
> *. . . And the continuous alternation of this never ceases . . .*[3]

How does this happen and how do these two states relate to each other? These are fundamental questions of origin, and the young child is our ardent Pre-Socratic philosopher. The world is in a constant dynamic state of becoming, of pure potentiality, but to these early philosophers, it is anchored in and by an unchanging fundamental Principle where being and truth reside. This could be Parmenides' position, but it would describe equally well the "position" of the Winnicottian infant. To the Pre-Socratics, the enduring Principle that is considered to be the "mother" of all and the fountain of being and truth, is a *thought*: "thinking is being" (το γαρ αυτο νοειν εστιν τε και ειναι) was Parmenides' thesis.[4] The psychoanalyst may see in the original Unity, in the One out of which everything originated, a reflection of the infant's phantasy[5] of a primordial fusional oneness-with-mother before the rupture and fracture of differentiation.

It is clear from the above that from the very beginning of Western thought there was a hierarchical arrangement of the two orders of reality. The invisible underlying unifying principle behind our quotidian variable sensory experiences is the locus of Reality with a capital R and is, further, the seat of Truth, of a "well-rounded truth" (Parmenides) that contrasts with the *doxa* of the forever changing manifold world of appearances.

We note, however, that Parmenides enjoins us to know both:

> *For you need to learn everything,*
> *Both the unshaken heart of well-rounded Truth*
> *As well as the opinions of the mortals which cannot be truly credited.*[6]

The challenge to maintain a bi-focal epistemological field, of necessity, introduces conflict.

The meta-physical Principle untouched by time had, as expected, a theological manifestation. This was the higher order of the immortal Olympian gods deciding the fate of the fleeting generations of mortals. In both instances, meta-physical and theological, what emerged was a dynamic (dis)equilibrium between two clashing realities that could define themselves only in opposition to each other: the eternal, immutable αρχη versus the flux of appearances, or the immortal divine versus the mortal human.

In the endless Herakleitian flow of things coming to be and passing away, the incomprehensible cessation of life, the sudden suspension of the living quality of humans, the fact of death, was obviously the prime enigma that confronted man and persistently demanded an answer. In the historical period of the West, the answer came in the concept of ψυχη, whose essential function was to assure continuity of being. Psyche was originally considered to be the principle of life, responsible for the breathing living human (from ψυχειν, an onomatopoetic verb indicating "to breathe").

In the *Iliad*, in Book XXIII, we have a remarkable scene. Achilles, inconsolable after the death of Patroklos, falls asleep on the shore, at the edge of the "deep-resounding sea." In his sleep Patroklos appears to him, exactly as he was in his former life, the same imposing stature, the same voice, and speaks to Achilles, imploring him not to delay his burial. Achilles, wishing to embrace his friend,

> *reached forth with loving hands, but he grasped nothing.*
> *The spirit, like smoke, rushed beneath the earth*
> *with a piercing cry.*

Achilles wakes up startled and, for the first time, ponders:

> *How strange! So there is a soul and a specter in the House of Hades*
> *Even though life is no more![7]*

Rohde[8] believed that such experiences of seeing the dead in a dream, together with the visions of devout worshippers in states of altered consciousness as, for example, in religious rituals, were probably at the root of the concept of psyche as autonomous from the body, and the basis of the belief that the dead continue to exist in another, invisible (αϊδης – Hades) universe, even after the death of the body. Patroklos is gone, but he continues to exist forever as an *eidolon* in a world hidden to us. The only difference between Achilles' conviction and Theodora's is on the level of verifiability. However, the psychic "gain" of Achilles' creative phantasy and Theodora's cognitive achievement is of the same magnitude.

Probably under the influence of Eastern beliefs traveling westward from India and Egypt, psyche was endowed with immortality.[9] Thus, psyche existing outside of time, immortal, like the Pre-Socratics' immutable enduring Reality behind the deceptive flux of the visible world, provided the necessary frame of stability in the *Weltanschauung* of the Ancients, which would allow the daring flights of the Greek mind that were to follow in the fifth and fourth century BCE.

The concept of the Homeric psyche had, of course, little to do with our modern concept of the psyche. It would not be inaccurate to say that the "psychological" dimension of the psyche was gradually grafted on to the Homeric principle of life primarily through the works of the lyric poets, such as Archilochos, Sappho and others in the centuries preceding Plato:

> *Soul, my soul, confused by hopeless troubles,*
> *look up and defend yourself against your enemies,*
> *setting a bold front against ambushes*
> *. . .*
> *And exult not openly if you prevail . . .*
> > (Archilochos)[10]

Or

> *I wish to say something to you, but shame prevents me.*
> > (Sappho)[11]

There is, unquestionably, something "poetic" in the post-Homeric concept of psyche – a quality of only peripheral interest to modern psychology in an era of dominant scientific positivism.

This raises, in passing, a fundamental question regarding the nature of psychoanalysis itself: are its deeper affinities to be found in the domain of poetry and metaphor, or in the domain of the neurosciences? We seem caught somewhere between Achilles and Theodora. Or, is this a spurious dilemma? Clearly, it is.

The concept of the psyche, thus, evolved over the next three centuries after Homer.[12] Through the influence of the poets, but also through that of some Pre-Socratic philosophers such as Alkmaion and Herakleitos, the seat of the faculties of thought, desire and volition were now located in the psyche. The result was that the Homeric psyche, endowed with immortality and progressively "psychologized," eventually gave rise to the

Platonic concept of a unitary composite psyche, the seat of eternal Ideas (ειδη). The Homeric *eidolon* evolved gradually into the Platonic *eidos*.

This was a momentous development because it represented a radical shift in the geography of meta-physical dualism: the polarity of a primal underlying Principle (αρχη) versus the flux of appearances, as well as the polarity of the immortal divine versus the finite human, were now *internalized* and placed inside the human psyche. The old hierarchical order was maintained such that the now composite psyche consisted of a higher "rational" part (λογιστικον) that corresponded to the eternal principle of Truth and an inferior "appetitive" part (επιθυμητικον) corresponding to the deceptive finite world of the senses. An intermediary part, the θυμοειδες, mediated between the two but leaned mostly on the side of the rational part. The primary significance of this shift in the geography of the dynamic field was that, now, the cosmic conflict between the two orders of reality was relocated in man's internal world. This marked the beginning of psychology in the modern sense.

However, this internalization also led to the introduction of *the tragic* in human affairs. The human agent was now divided between a divine and a perishable part, as her world was split between a visible transience and an invisible enduring universe, source of all vitality and truth. The human being was seen as "chained" in that "in-between" dark space that Plato depicts with ingenuity and poetic elegance in his Myth of the Cave.[13] The confrontation, the *agon* (αγων), between gods and men will be from now on between two agencies within the human soul, ultimately between mind and body.

These were portentous movements that indicated the beginning of a significant re-location of the seat of human action: the prime mover of human action began its descent from the heights of Mount Olympus to the depths of the human soul. This marked the historic evolution from *Mythos* to *Logos*. Man was to become the "measure of all things" and carries hence the weight of his moral dilemmas, impasses and choices.

There is an inherent ontological *conservatism* in living matter that resists change insofar as change ultimately means the inversion of *bios* to *thanatos*. The above ideological theologico-philosophic developments in Greek Antiquity, which are centered around the belief in the existence of an enduring underlying primary agency/substance, were primarily motivated by the human need for stability and continuity – the continuity of being. It is the primal fear of *loss* – loss of the object, entailing loss of the subject – that generated such beliefs. The wish to conserve the *status quo* and avert change insofar as it signifies death is paramount in human affairs.

Thus, the world of the Ancients came to be structured along two planes of reality, of truth, of morality and of aesthetic beauty. There was, on the one hand, the underlying, eternal, true but not immediately given to the senses, psychic world of the permanent ειδη, the independently existing innate entities that give form to human experience; on the other hand, there was the lived world of external experience, a shifting world of transience and loss. The "Real" was a resident of the former.

Over 2000 years later, Freud[14] would advance the reflection on the ancient paradigm of constructing reality along two planes and refer to the essential aspects of the obscure underlying world of truth and ultimate reality as the Unconscious, our *Andere Schauplatz*, in contradistinction to what appears on the superficial visible stage. He considered this *other stage* as the locus of "psychic reality" and as the indomitable force that determines the events occurring on the daily observable stage. He showed that it is only through *another eye* that we can be granted a glimpse of this other stage of the real: Teiresias' "blind eye."

In this manner of "seeing," the lost object – product of unstoppable change – is always there, time-less, eternal. The "dead," absent object returns – even though disguised. It returns as a ghost, as an Idea, as a spurious presence, a kind of thought, a mental image. It is insistent, and it is indelible – or there is no life.

Melanie Klein and her followers went further in their consideration of the two worlds. The external observable world is not merely determined by the forces of the inner psychic world, it is, at its earliest stages, *created* by these forces. Kleinian thought, here, points to a long tradition of Idealist thinkers from Plato to Kant and Fichte whose haunting nightmare is, inescapably, solipsism. The infant, according to Klein, projects her internal objects and relationships and thus populates and activates the external world.[15] It is noteworthy that Plato, in the *Republic*, presents a view that is consonant with Klein's notion of the external world as a reflection of the internal, even though in Plato the relation leans more towards parallelism. Socrates' aim is to study the human psyche; to facilitate his task Socrates proposes to shift his attention to a larger scale, that of society, where he believes the same forces operate as in the inner world, obeying the same dynamic relational pattern; he can thus have a clearer glimpse of what goes on in the psyche. The outside world is a mirror of the psychic world. However, Plato, the psychologist, was all too aware of the fact that, even though the pattern, the forces and the "players" operating in the two fields were the same, the two worlds were, in fact, discrepant in their final configuration. A harmonious relation was posited as the ideal aim.

Parmenides' injunction on the desirability of knowing both sides of the truth, we must conclude, articulated and proposed a herculean human task. The "well-rounded truth" can only be attained through its negation by the "opinions of the mortals" (according to a figure-ground Gestalt). However, if being is "being with" – as the Kleinians insisted – the *I* is obliged to eye *two* sides at the same time and to invest simultaneously two discrepant and conflicting worlds. Moreover, it is free to repudiate the existence of either – at the price of madness, or death:

> *I, Ajax, victim of a double deception*
> (Heiner Müller)[16]

Here, we enter the domain of theater.

Psychoanalysis has taught us that humans tend to deal with psychic trauma by repeating it in some form. Theater appears to be a sort of "repetition" of something. However, a repetition of what? It is said to be an "imitation" (Aristotle) and, without specifying for the moment what it is exactly that theater attempts to imitate, it is clear that imitation means doubling. The resulting theatrical situation is, accordingly, one in which we find ourselves spectators of two realities: some unspecified "original" and another – its double – unfolding in front of our eyes.

It would seem that the theatrical act attempts to deal with the inexorable strain of a divided human experience torn between two opposing realities. Theater institutes a two-stage universe and situates itself at the border between the experience of ordinary daily (as opposed to "nightly"?) reality, on the one hand, and the experience of a sort of invisible, "immaterial" reality, on the other – a reality that exists in a space *behind* the stage setting. These two realities are engaged in a never-ending αγων.

The *mimesis*[17] that theater operates is, in effect, a *meta-phora* (μεταφορα means "transfer") of some obscure "other world" onto the visible stage. The "other" self and its world are reflected – but through a distorting and clouded mirror – and appear in front of us in the coordinates of common experience. In this act, the self is reflected and reflecting on its ontological schism. The nature of the "original" remains, of course, undetermined and, perhaps, undeterminable. All human intellectual endeavor has aimed at the elucidation of this eluding "primal" reality. This marks theater, ultimately, as a meta-physical enterprise and as a search for the invisible. *Absence* is at the very core of the theatrical event: theater could be said, in the end, to be a *theoria* ("view") of absence, a vision of the invisible. It is founded on a dualism whose one pole is suspended in the Void. This is so because the fundamental duality underlying all dualities is the polarity of *living–dead*. This makes all theater a *theatron* (viewing instrument) of the dead (*Αδης/Α-ιδης* means "in-visible"), a theater of death.

The particular interest of the psychoanalyst in the theater is not entirely surprising. There are certain common forces and a similar dynamic that define both the psychoanalytic setting and the theatrical setting. It was Breuer's patient Fraulein Anna O. – the first analytic patient, even though only by proxy – who spoke to Breuer of her "private theater,"[18] the theater of her mind, referring to her fantasies and daydreaming in that "other stage." Since then, much has been written of the essentially theatrical structure of the psychoanalytic process.[19] According to this view, analysand and analyst are, in effect, playwrights, actors and spectators, as well as directors of events unfolding on two doubled (analyst/analysand) and mutually mirrored psychic stages, each forming a "screen" for the other. Behind the events occupying the "visible" (audible) analytic stage, there are the uncanny occurrences of a concealed inaudible universe.

As for the question of death in all this, psychoanalytic theory has accorded death a central place since the publication of Freud's *Beyond the Pleasure Principle* in 1920.[20] In its evolved version the death drive has become the cornerstone of Kleinian and post-Kleinian psychoanalytic thinking. Moreover, death constituted the core of ancient tragedy that played a significant role in the emergence of psychoanalytic theory.

Adopting a psychoanalytic perspective and using the Western theatrical experience as a springboard, the aim of the present work is to inquire into the possible relation of theater (understood as an elemental human activity) to death (as a violent ontological loss preserved in a universal primal phantasy) and to propose a manner of conceptualizing the nature of their relationship.

Part I will examine the emergence of the theatrical phenomenon and will offer a hypothesis that links it to an unconscious phantasy of a primordial birth–death experience. Part II will focus more specifically on the Theater of Death of Tadeusz Kantor as an illustration of the views proposed in Part I.

Notes

1 B. Snell, *Die Ausdrücke Für der Begriff des Wissens in der Vorplatonischen Philosophie* (Berlin: Weidmann, 1924).
2 G.S. Kirk and J.E. Raven, *The Presocratic Philosophers* (Cambridge U. Press, 1971), 235.
3 *Ibid.*, 326.
4 *Ibid.*, 269.
5 Phantasy is spelled with *ph* throughout this book to indicate *unconscious* phantasy as distinguished from conscious fantasy. See S. Isaacs, "The nature and function of phantasy," *Int. J. Psycho-Anal.*, 1948: 73–97.
6 Kirk and Raven (1971), 267.
7 Homer, *Homeri Opera*, eds. D.B. Munro and T.W. Allen (London: Oxford Classical Texts, 1920), *Iliad*, XXIII: 104. Translation by the author.
8 E. Rohde, *Psyche*, trans. H.B. Willis (London, 1895).

9   See J. Bremmer, *The Early Greek Concept of the Soul* (Princeton, NJ: Princeton U. Press, 1983).

10 *Greek Elegy and Iambus*, trans. J.M. Edmonds (Cambridge, MA: Harvard U. Press, 1979), v. 2.

11 *Greek Lyric*, trans. D.A. Campbell (Cambridge, MA: Harvard U. Press, 1990), v. 1.

12 See Bremmer (1983). Also, B. Snell, *The Discovery of the Mind* (New York: Dover Publications, 1982).

13 Plato, *The Republic*, trans. F.M. Cornford (Oxford U. Press, 1945), 227–235.

14 S. Freud, "The Interpretation of Dreams," *The Standard Edition of the Complete Psychological Works of Sigmund Freud*, ed. and trans. J. Strachey (London: Hogarth Press, 1981), 4: 48.

15 M. Klein, "The importance of symbol-formation in the development of the ego," *Int. J. Psycho-Anal.*, 1930: 24–39.

16 Heiner Müller, *Die Gedichte* (Frankfurt am Main: Suhrkamp, 1998), 1: 294.

17 S.H. Butcher, *Aristotle's Theory of Poetry and Fine Art* (New York: Dover Publications, 1951), 1449b24.

18 Freud, *S.E.* 2: 22.

19 H. Loewald, "Psychoanalysis as an art and the fantasy character of the psychoanalytic situation," *J. Amer. Psychoanal. Assn.*, 1975: 277–299. Also, J. McDougall, *Theaters of the Mind: Illusion and Truth on the Psychoanalytic Stage* (New York: Brunner-Routledge, 1991).

20 Freud, *S.E.* 18: 3–64.

Part I

1   Dionysos and the tragic

Every epoch believes itself to be the end of history. We, unquestionably, focus more passionately on ends than on beginnings. History advances oblivious to human loss yet mobilized by it. The new emerges out of mourning for the old. The chorus of "mourners" is always led by the poet who positions her/himself at the border between two worlds. Thus, Euripides, an old man in exile – exiled from his time, not only geographically – takes up the *kalamos* to write down his last play in the wild forests of Macedonia. It is a nightmare, a cry of protest, an act of despair, perhaps even an act of revenge. The scene opens on a ruined landscape, smitten by divine fire, a smoldering thunder-blasted tomb. It is a mother's tomb, a mother that was struck by lightning and gave birth to her baby, a birth before its due time (time always runs ahead of being). All this by a clear mountain spring that flows quietly into a river. Birth–death, violent rupture and a tranquil stream of soothing continuity seize the spectator in the first eight lines of the *Bacchae*.[1] Moreover, something else: "Here I come disguised," declares the son now re-appearing on the scene, returning to the deadly place of his birth.

"Many are the forms of the Daemon," the chorus will conclude 1388 lines later – clearly two: living, dead, both in disguise.

The *Bacchae* is a play whose intriguing seductive appeal few stage directors have been able to resist – and it has proven to be the Waterloo of many. It has been called a meta-tragedy,[2] a tragedy about tragedy, a play about the very nature of theater. It tells of the powers of the divine – powers of creation and destruction – the might of Dionysos, whose terrifying hegemony no-one may contest.

Dionysos has been the subject of several lost tragedies, e.g., Aeschylus' *Pentheus, Bassaridae* and the *Lykurgos* trilogy, but it is only Euripides' *Bacchae* that has survived in its entirety. In the *Bacchae*, Segal claims, "Euripides uses the figure of Dionysos as a god of the tragic mask to reflect on the paradoxical nature of tragedy itself."[3] It will be argued here that it is the paradoxical nature of *all* theater that is dealt with in the *Bacchae*.

Although it has not been without challenges,[4] the prevailing view is that tragedy as a genre is intimately linked with Dionysos and the ritual practices of his early worshippers. The historical evidence for this comes from Herodotus[5] and, importantly, from Aristotle's account in his *Poetics*.[6] Aristotle's theory of the origins of tragedy must be taken seriously, insofar as he was chronologically closest to the facts (even though removed from them by about two centuries) and it is likely that he had access to sources no longer available to us. Aristotle claims that tragedy emerged as an "improvisation" that was started by the "leaders of the dithyramb"[7] and evolved gradually until it reached its final form. Dithyramb was the song of the followers of Dionysos accompanying their frenzied, ecstatic dances. We read, for example, Archilochos, the seventh-century iambic poet, who is boasting that he knows "how to lead off the fair song of Dionysos, the dithyramb, when my wits are thunder-struck with wine."[8] In fact, "dithyramb" was used as an epithet for the god.

A crucial question that confronts us is the exact nature of the "improvisation" that Aristotle mentions as the first step leading to the development of tragedy, a step taken by the leader of the dithyramb. What exactly did it involve? We shall return to this important question. What is, however, generally accepted is that the origins of tragedy are traceable back to the early Dionysian satyr chorus and the associated dithyramb hymns sung in honor of Dionysos. In view of this, a closer look at the god of tragedy as we see him in the only surviving tragedy in which he is the central figure may throw some light on the nature of tragedy itself and on the nature of the tragic in particular.

The traditional belief held Dionysos to be a newcomer to Greek soil, surreptitiously invading from the north and challenging Apollo, the Greek god of light, clarity and aesthetic order. This, however, has been shown to be unfounded following recent archeological evidence. At the end of the nineteenth century, Rohde,[9] in advocating Dionysos to be an element foreign to Greek culture, was expressing the dominant idealizing view of his time that regarded the Greeks as a purified culture of order, reason and harmony. Basing himself on Herodotus' claims[10] and on the fact that the god is hardly present in Homer, Rohde maintained that the barbarian Thracian god was belatedly introduced to Apollonian Greece and that this was done against great local resistance. Dionysos – following this view – became gradually "Hellenized and humanized," eventually taking his place side by side with Apollo in Greek religious life. This was shown in the pediments of the Delphic temple: the east classic pediment was occupied by Apollo and the Muses, whereas the Western classic pediment showed Dionysos and his maenadic *thyiads*. Wilamowitz,[11] too, was of the opinion that the establishment of worship of Dionysos in Greece could not have taken place before 700 BCE. All this, however, had to be revised when excavations in the island of Keos brought to light a sanctuary of Dionysos dating back to the fifteenth century BCE. In addition, evidence from deciphered Linear B tablets from Pylos indicates that the worship of Dionysos was already established in Mycenaean times. It would seem, therefore, that, alongside the worship of Apollo, Greek society had, as early as the Late Helladic period, maintained a space for the observance of the *ek-static*,[12] the mystical, the irrational, the uncanny and the *other*worldly represented by the illusive god. Peisistratus' political acumen led him to found, in the sixth century, the Great Dionysia festival to honor the god that "brings to wretched humans . . . sleep and oblivion from daily sorrows."[13]

It was during the five-day festival of the Great Dionysia, or City Dionysia, celebrated in the spring month of *Elaphebolion*, that tragedies were performed and trophies awarded to the best tragedians. Tragedies were performed, also, at another festival in honor of Dionysos, the Lenaia, which took place earlier in the year, in the month of *Gamelion*, i.e., the month of weddings. The performance of tragedies as a core component of Dionysian festivals adds support to the theory that tragedy, both regarding its origins and to its form, had a deep connection with the god's worship.

In the formative shadow of the Aristotelian legacy, Nietzsche,[14] proclaiming himself to be "the last disciple of the philosopher Dionysus," developed, in his *The Birth of Tragedy From the Spirit of Music* that appeared in 1872, the theme of the Dionysian origins of tragedy, linking it to the primitive forces governing the god's fusional satyr chorus chanting the dithyramb. The book sold initially only 625 copies and damaged Nietzsche's academic career irreparably, but its subsequent influence has been immense.

The ritual origins of tragedy were given a new emphasis and a novel interpretation by a group of British scholars (J.E. Harrison, F.M. Cornford and G. Murray) at the beginning of the twentieth century. Influenced by W.R. Smith's theories about ritual and myth and J.G. Frazer's evolutionary anthropological theories that were quite popular at the time, these so-called "Cambridge Ritualists" believed Dionysos to be, in effect, a Year God (*eniautos daimon*)[15] that represented the natural cycle of death and rebirth. They held, accordingly, that tragedy arose from spring vegetation rituals celebrating the rebirth of the Year Spirit identified with Dionysos. Although the Year God theory of the origin of tragedy has been criticized for lack of evidence,[16] the theory's refutation has not challenged the direct link of tragedy to Dionysos and his rituals.

Looking at Euripides' play now, we see Dionysos disguised as a traveler arriving at his native city, Thebes. Thebes is ruled by his cousin

Pentheus who refuses to recognize Dionysos' divine status and scoffs at his rituals. Intent on initiating the Thebans to his mysteries, Dionysos drives the women of Thebes to the hills in Bacchic frenzy, while his retinue of Asiatic women sing the story of the god's miraculous violent double birth, first from his mortal mother's womb and later from his father Zeus' thigh. The Stranger cleverly seduces Pentheus to stealthily watch the maenads' "secret dances" in the wild – sights "pleasurable and repulsive" – dressing him up as a bacchant in order not to be recognized. Once dressed up Pentheus declares seeing double, beholding *two* suns and *two* Thebes, to which the Stranger responds "Now you see as you should." Alas, the eager spectator of the women's mysterious exploits becomes *himself* part of a primordial sacred act, as "his flesh is broken asunder" by entranced mother and his body is left "divided." When she recovers from her ecstatic orgy, Agave bewails: "Oh *penthos* [mourning grief] immeasurable! Oh murder by these wretched hands!" The god finally appears in his true guise speaking of the folly of trying to eschew "what is of necessity." The play ends with the chorus meditating:

> *Manifold are the forms of the Daimon*
> *Thus developed this thing.*[17]

This *thing*. The thing ($\pi\rho\alpha\gamma\mu\alpha$) is what the spectator saw – $\pi\rho\alpha\gamma\mu\alpha$, in its etymological sense is a "deed," i.e., an act here depicted on stage. However, it is also what the spectator could not see, ultimately the "thing-in-itself," the *other* deed, of which the visible thing is an "imitation" ($\mu\iota\mu\eta\sigma\iota\varsigma$). To get a glimpse of the *other* deed, the spectator/Pentheus, curiously spying at the "secret dances," must become himself the "thing" to be seen, both subject and object of the secret deed. This necessitates an ontological rupture and a mimetic doubling that undoes itself. Here we have the foundational dynamic of theater and, at the same time, an insurmountable meta-physical block inherent to any possibility of $\theta\varepsilon\alpha\tau\rho\sigma\nu$. Theater is, ultimately, what *cannot* be theater ($\theta\varepsilon\alpha\sigma\mu\alpha\iota$ means "I view," "I gaze"). However, more of this later.

The possibility of an impossible theater, however, can only arise within the frame of a theatrical situation or setting: a spectator face-to-face with a spectacle. The theatrical setting is one of constraint (to see what is visible, *in ludere*) and of freedom (to "see" what can*not* be seen). The first question, therefore, regarding Dionysos concerns his connection with the construction of theater's defining *bi-focal field*.

Gods create in their own likeness, and no less would be expected of the "di-morphous" god, as Dionysos is called by Diodorus, imprinting his dual identity on his *enthousiastic* ("inhabited by the god") followers.

"Who is this god?" asks Pentheus in the *Bacchae*. The Stranger answers: "Whosoever he wishes to be." Dionysos is the *ek-static* god of altered states, of multiple realities and of multiple identities. A human god of two births, he is both masculine and feminine, both beast and god. He appears to the Thebans in disguise as an Other, while his "double," Pentheus, disguises himself as a *bacche* in order to be the spectator/actor of the "pleasurable and horrible" secret acts of his mother and the other women of Thebes. However, he himself becomes the outwitted actor pathetically acted upon in the primordial and terminal drama of his existence, with his dismemberment (*sparagmos*) by his own mother, in front of the Athenian spectators whose tragic double he represents. The masked god presents himself here as a "re-presentation" of himself, as the prototypical actor, positioning himself ambiguously between two realities, between the divine and the human, between sanity and madness. The *Bacchae* unfolds as a telescoped series of plays-within-plays, of self-multiplying mirror images where, unavoidably, the gaze of the spectator's eye eventually returns to the *I*. At the very center of these revolving and receding mirror images and identities, however, there is a scene of mutilation, of a primordial violent rupture which provides the core of the entire multifaceted spectacle. This is the event, the πρᾶγμα, of maternal *sparagmos*. This deed echoes the original ritual sacrifice of the animal/god at the altar (θυμέλη), a ritual sacrifice repeated at the beginning of each Dionysia festival, before the performances began, as the god's priest would sacrifice an animal at the altar situated at the center of the orchestra.

Dionysos appears as the god of a double reality, of alternate selves, of two opposing natures freely sliding into each other across an imperceptible boundary. He is the vegetation god of sweet tendrils, of ivy-staves dripping honey, of nature's life-giving nourishment and serene rapture (ll. 699–711), a "most gentle" (l. 861) god, soothing life's daily sorrows and offering rest and oblivion from grief when men are filled with the vine's flowing sap (ll. 280–285). Thus, the messenger describes (ll. 677 ff) a peaceful pastoral scene on the hillside: the god's devotees, women "young, old, unwed virgins lie"

> *. . . sleeping with bodies relaxed,*
> *some leaning their backs against a fir tree's foliage,*
> *others among oak leaves resting their heads on the ground,*
> *carelessly . . .*[18]

Then, as the first rays of the rising sun begin to warm the earth, they awake letting their rich locks of hair fall on their shoulders:

A miracle of harmonious order to behold.

However, at the same time, Dionysos is the ruthless chthonic sovereign of the darkest forces of savagery, of the unspeakable horror of primeval cruelty, a god "most dreadful" (l. 861) to wretched humans. The two scenes in the *Bacchae* (ll. 734–747 and ll. 1122–1141) of fierce, bloodthirsty mutilation by the same women just described seized by Dionysian frenzy are two of the most potent frightful passages spoken in Greek literature:

> *They* [the maenads] *attacked the grazing heifers*
> *with hand that bore no steal.*
> *And one you could have seen holding asunder in her hands*
> *a tight-uddered young bellowing heifer;*
> *while others were tearing full-grown cows to pieces.*
> *You could have seen ribs, or a cloven hoof,*
> *being hurled to and fro; and these hung*
> *dripping under the fir trees, all mixed with blood.*
> *Bulls that were arrogant before, with rage in their horns,*
> *stumbled to the ground,*
> *borne down by the countless hands of girls.*
> *The garments of flesh were drawn apart more quickly*
> *than you close the lids over your royal eyes.*[19]

This is what the messenger reports to Pentheus.

Later on, the messenger will describe Pentheus' own savage mutilation in the hands of his mother:

> *Discharging foam from her mouth*
> *and rolling her eyes all around,*
> *her mind not as it should be,*
> *was possessed by the Bacchic god*
> *. . .*
> *Grasping his left arm below the elbow,*
> *and setting her foot against the unhappy man's ribs,*
> *she tore his shoulder out, not by her normal strength,*
> *but the god gave a special ease to her hands.*
> *Ino was wrecking the other side of him,*
> *breaking his flesh, and Autonoe and the whole mob of bacchants*
> *laid hold on him; all gave voice at once –*
> *he moaning with what breath was left in him,*
> *they screaming in triumph.*
> *One was carrying a forearm,*

another a foot with the boot still on;
the ribs were being laid bare by the tearing;
and each of the women, with hands all bloody,
was playing ball with Pentheus' flesh.
The body lies scattered, part under blind rocks,
part among the deep-wooded foliage of the forest,
no easy search;
and the poor head,
which his mother just then seized in her hands,
she fixed on the point of her thyrsus . . .[20]

Here, the *other* face of the masked god of merriment (Eros) emerges showing him to be the god of brutal bodily dismemberment, of bodily fractures and ontological divisions (Thanatos).

Yet, the god of a sundered reality and violent fragmentation, Dionysos is, also, the god of *fluid boundaries*, of paradoxical links between contradictory realities. He is known as *Lysios*, the "loosener" of rigid boundaries, the god of inexplicably shifting interchangeable identities, wavering between reality and illusion, between the human and the divine, between sanity and madness, in the same way that he slides between savagery and tenderness. Rupture–merge: is this an obsessively repeated compensatory attempt to repair an irreparable ontological fracture?

Looking at the obverse of Dionysos' "mask," i.e., Pentheus the anti-Dionysos, we can get a clearer view of the god. Pentheus is the tragic hero that refuses to be tragic. His Aristotelian "flaw" (*hamartia*) is that of denying duality and the existence of multiple fluid and contradictory realities and insisting on a uni-dimensional monolithic rational static universe. Intolerant of altered and alternative realities, what Pentheus is disavowing is the original generative chaos and the differentiating violence that led to individuation and consequent multiformity. One might say that he refuses to acknowledge his identity as only a *fragment*, as the product of a division, a breakup of what was once a totality but is no more. He, the "mournful" Pentheus (*penthein* means "to mourn"), toils to avoid mourning for his state of incompleteness, a mourning, however, that is necessary for the grounding of a cohesive identity. Dionysos/Stranger confronts him early on (l. 506):

You know not your life, nor your acts, nor who you are.

A firm sense of identity is grounded in the past. Pentheus seems to "forget" what cannot be forgotten and so it returns to destroy him. Refusing to be "divinely mad" (Plato, *Phaedrus*),[21] he is struck with madness which is, ironically, a violent restitution of reason. When he allows himself to be *another*, i.e., to step out (*ek-stasis*) of his unitary universe and admit the existence of *other* realities, he exclaims (ll. 918–919), as we saw above:

> *Aha! I now see two suns and a double Thebes.*

Which prompts the Stranger to point to him (ll. 947–948):

> *Before your mind was not healthy,*
> *but now* [that you see double] *your mind is as it should be.*

Unable to mourn and to deal with the depressive anxieties (Klein) related to the recognition of the multiform, fragmented and fluid character of reality, Pentheus seeks to protect himself from his mother's aggression by identifying with her, dressing up as a maenad and taking on "*the same form as Kadmus' daughter*" – a strategy which, as we saw, failed tragically. Yet, by adopting the identity of a maenad and, also, by becoming the secret spectator of his mother's orgies, Pentheus is unwittingly assuming his painful duality, and this on two accounts (by becoming the Other and by becoming an observer of the Other/self). Here we have the quintessential dynamic of the theatrical setting. Thus, he who had refused to "remember" his state of being only a fragment is brutally dis-membered, as his past re-asserts itself in a perpetual present.

The "play" had begun with a dead mother's *mnema* (l. 6), a memorial to a catastrophic originary event, and ends with the non-*mnema* of the murdered son. Pentheus has no *mnema* (his members dispersed) because his tomb is in his mother's body and his *penthos* remains unacknowledged, hence interminable. He has no *mnema* because in disavowing his pre-historic rupture and his present state of incompletion Pentheus is a man without memory.

Dionysos, we conclude, is the god of violent fragmentation and duality, a duality that causes man's "tragic dissonance"[22] with himself. This duality manifests the violent scission of human reality, the dehiscence of the primordial oneness of being. We suggest that this is what constitutes *the tragic*.[23]

Duality presents itself as an ontological *a priori* for humans, condemning man to un-resolvable Kantian antinomies and constituting an ineluctable precondition of self-consciousness and human thought. Disrupting the cohesion of being provides the ground for ambiguity and paradox and determines the nature of Dionysian truth as, of necessity, enigmatic because it is always partial and affirms itself through self-negation (cf. Hegel's *Aufhebung*).[24]

In this manner, the meta-physical ground of the dichotomous space of theater is constructed and is now ready to be occupied by its ghosts on either side of a mirror. Aristotle defines *aenigma* as an impossible link,[25] as the mixing of immiscibles. The god of tragedy is, indeed, the enigmatic god *par excellence*, the conjunction of opposites, the god of contradictory yet interchangeable realities. Reality is enigmatic because of its admixture with illusion, so that – as the god's followers pointedly proclaim – "wisdom is not wisdom" (*Bacchae*, l. 395). This is so because truth *slides* between its various fragments. These fragments affirm that behind the enigmatic conjunction of opposites lies the tragic dis-junction (*sparagmos*) of the identical. The god of tragedy is a god of primordial violence.

So, it seems that it is in this ill-defined universe of binary opposites, of chaotic *ek-static* states, of altered perception, of sacred violence, of ambiguity and masked realities, that we have to search for the roots of tragedy, and, indeed, the roots of theater in general.

The duality of the masked god that results from the violent schism that he embodies brings into focus the dark side of the god of revelry and phallic procreative powers. A look at the festivals in his honor reveals Dionysos to be the chthonic god of the dead, Persephone's son, as he was considered in the Orphic tradition (which is further corroborated by the presence of satyrs in tomb reliefs). In Herodotos,[26] too, we hear of Dionysos as "the Ruler of the Lower World." In his festivals, the god of theater makes his final appearance as the "Lord of the Souls." The Anthesteria took place in the spring "Flower Month" (Aνθηστηριον). It was a festival to celebrate the opening of the jars of the new wine that had been pressed in the Fall. However, it was, in effect, a festival of the dead. The festival was also referred to as the "Older Dionysia" in contrast to the Great Dionysia that was introduced only in the sixth century.[27] In the Anthesteria, the pots of the new wine were opened on the first day of a three-day festival. On the second day, ghosts of the dead (masked mummers) invaded and haunted the city. This day was called "polluted day" (μιαρα ημερα). The doors of the houses were painted black to keep the ghosts out. Inside, men, in utter silence, would participate in a ritual drinking contest. This was probably a reference to the meal offered by the Athenians to Orestes after he killed his mother. However, it may have also been a reference to a related myth about the murder of Ikarios who had brought wine to Attica after he had been shown how to make wine by Dionysos: the villagers thought that Ikarios had given them a deadly poison and so killed him. In either case, these aetiological myths point to the profound association between wine and blood, between revelry and death. The drinking contest of the Anthesteria had the characteristics of a sacrificial meal after a bloody sacrifice. Whose sacrifice? Was the new wine drunk by the worshippers the blood of the sacrificed god Dionysos who had been torn apart (as the grapes were torn to make wine)? The parallels with Christian rites are obvious, pointing to the fact that such ancient customs stem from deep-rooted fears and anxieties related to universal unconscious phantasies. To close the circle, the last day of the festival was dominated by the procreative side of the Anthesteria, in which a sacred marriage of the "Queen" and Dionysos (represented by his idol?) took place, alluding to the god's union with Ariadne.

Thus, in the Anthesteria, the themes of generative rites were inter-mingled with death rites. The scene of merriment and frolic was soon infused with panic and fright. A disorganizing invasion of the unfamiliar, uncanny alien spirits terrorized the townspeople and "polluted" them with their "otherness" until they were expelled from the community ("*Out you Keres*") and order was restored. *Exeunt.*

The Agrionia was another old festival in honor of Dionysos, in which – Burkert tells us[28] – "the power of Dionysos appears more savagely." This, too, appears to have been a festival of the dead, as attested by Hesychius.[29] In Argos, this festival was called "Festivity for the Dead" (Νεκυσια). The myth surrounding the Agrionia was that of the daughters of Minyas and involved filicide. Refusing to worship Dionysos, the Minyads were punished by being seized by divine mania; they drew lots as to who would make a sacrifice to the god. Leukippe drew the ritual lot and sacrificed her own son tearing him to pieces. During the festival, which took place at night, women seized by Dionysian frenzy would flee to the hills calling for the god for three nights. There were likely nocturnal sacrifices to the god, possibly including a human sacrifice by Dionysos' priest.

As already noted, Dionysos had a pronounced feminine side, his world being essentially a feminine world. His followers were women, but it was not the Dionysian *erotic* element that drove these women. Rather, they were imbued with a powerful *maternal* instinct. They were mothers tenderly holding in their arms and nursing newborns, fawns, deer, even wolf-cubs and other wild animals. Suddenly, however, they would be transformed into wild, raw flesh-eating beasts (*omophagia*) tearing apart their prey, driven by forces of death. This savage side of the god's cult is a recurring theme in myths related to Dionysos. The vicious tearing apart of the body gave Dionysos the epithet of *anthroporraistes* ("he who tears humans apart"). He himself had been the victim of *sparagmos* as a child, torn to pieces by the Titans at the command of Mother Goddess Hera; and, most importantly, at the time of his birth, he had been violently torn out his mother's womb struck by Zeus' thunder. Also, Orpheus, whose identity overlaps with that of Dionysos, was ripped apart by raving Thracian women. There is a host of mothers, followers of Dionysos, who tore their children apart when they were seized by Dionysian frenzy.

This was the case of Leukippe, of Procne, of the women of Argos, of the daughters of Proitos, the daughters of Pandion and others. This antithetical image of motherhood as both tenderly nourishing and savagely murdering their young raises fundamental questions. Mothers, at the peak of ecstasy, tear off the flesh of their own children, kill the life they have created. It is as if gentle nurturing maternal care is inseparable from wild maternal destructiveness. Life-giving forces and forces of annihilation co-exist and even coincide under the sign of Dionysos.

This dark side of Dionysos and his deep relation to the world of the dead is further attested by his connection with Orpheus and Orphic mysteries. As already noted, Orpheus, too, who had descended to Hades to bring Euridice back, had been torn to pieces by Thracian maenads, as Dionysos/Zagreus had been by the Titans. Herodotos[30] points to a link between Bacchic and Orphic cults noting that both of these cults prescribe burying the dead in linen shrouds rather than woolen ones. A gold leaf found at Hipponion in 1969 and dating to the time of Herodotos gives us further information about Orphic and Dionysian cults and their common beliefs in the afterlife. We read in this leaf that the initiates (*mystai* and *bacchoi*), walking along the sacred way in the House of Hades, are enjoined to stop and drink "the cool water flowing from the Lake of Recollection."[31] This flowing water of memory and recollection can re-establish and maintain the broken link between the living and the dead. We meet here, again, the Dionysian theme of a radical rupture side by side with the injunction to link the irreconcilable opposites that follow – memories returning show the way (a message not lost on psychoanalysis). The Orphic mystic aims to enter into a state fashioned by the incomprehensible interchangeability, indeed the inextricable *one-ness*, of life and death. In the sacred dances of Dionysos' followers, this state is achieved through the ecstatic union (fusion) of the mortal dancer with the immortal god (*entousiasmos*). In their frenzied gyrations, life and death merged in the orgiastic delirium of the creation of the new. Life at its "manic" extreme comes to coincide with death. Otto[32] aptly points out that divinities of birth and procreation are intimately connected, if not identical, with divinities of death. We are reminded that festivities for the dead are frequently in the spring, i.e., at the time of nature's rebirth.

No-one has expressed the paradoxical fusional intermingling of life and death more succinctly than that master of riddles, Herakleitos the "obscure":

> *Immortal mortals, mortal immortals, these living the death of those, those dying the life of these.*[33]

In Herakleitos' characteristic fundamental ambiguity this fragment can be read in two (or more) different ways, depending which word is stressed – a subtlety lost in translation:

> *Mortal immortals, immortal mortals, these living the death of those, those dying the life of these.*

In the first reading, the immortality of the mortals is asserted, while in the second reading the mortality of the gods is proclaimed; in either case, each is said to live [in] the other's death and to die [in] the other's life.

Opposites may be interchangeable mirror images of each other – a theme dear to Herakleitos – their existence, however, as he himself stresses, is the consequence of universal strife (*polemos*) and violence, and it is this dimension that characterizes Dionysos' deeper nature. Herakleitos, to whom we owe the oldest testimony regarding Dionysian mystics (even though it is in Homer's *Iliad*, in VI: 132, that we find the oldest mention of Dionysos), is unequivocal about the identity of Dionysos: the god of phallic procreative rituals is the god of the dead. Herakleitos' surviving fragment reads:

> *Hades and Dionysos,*
> *for whom they rave and celebrate Lenaean rites,*
> *are one and the same.*[34]

This reflects the ultimate ground of Dionysos' ontological duality, i.e., life–death.

The *Bacchae* ends with the chorus' concluding line "*Thus unfolded this deed.*" If we regard the *Bacchae* as a reflection on the deeper nature of tragedy, as has been claimed by many, the nature of this Dionysian "deed" would indicate the essential core of tragedy and the tragic in human affairs. The deed in question, the culminating and central moment of the play, is clearly the filial *sparagmos*, the dismemberment of the Pentheus' body by his mother. We propose to consider this act as the re-presentation of the painful events that mark the time of the infant's original separation from mother, experienced as violent fragmentation and equated with death. Here is the origin and cause of human ontological division, the rupture or scission of being and of reality that constitutes the essence of the tragic and casts a tragic character on human life. The generative split of the primeval bio-psychic unity, or Oneness (the originally fused mother–infant), that gave birth to the individual *I* as a separate entity[35] condemned it to be forever – in part at least – external to itself, "unhoused in being," in Steiner's apposite expression referring to the "absolute tragic."[36] The *I* is, thus, *inherently* tragic. It is constructed around a gap and defined by self-alienation. Insofar as this division results in a self and its own absence (it is a part of the *self* that is lost after the "break" of differentiation), the gap can be conceived as an insurmountable parallax gap inherent in the One, rather than the result of the polar opposition of two independent sides.[37] On the cultural evolutionary level, the tragic appears at the point of emergence of *homo sapiens*, specifically when *homo* becomes *sapiens* of his/her ontological rupture and alienation and capable of self-consciousness.[38]

We hypothesize that the primal mother–child split that takes place at the time of the somatic and psychic birth of the individual is experienced by the archaic undifferentiated living unit as a trauma[39] at the deepest level of being. This trauma constituted as a "lack of being,"[40] will form the nucleus of the nascent *I* and will condemn it to an interminable longing for re-union. It is as if the breaking-up of a cosmic One that leads to the birth of the individual is a crime against Nature's equilibrium because it introduces conflict. The existential rift that led from One to Two will always be a source of profound anxiety, as the poet asserts:

> *But two was never a number*
> *because it is agony and its shadow,*
> *because it is the proof of another infinite which is not its own*
> *and it is the walls of death*
> *and the endless punishment of the new resurrection.*
> (Lorca, *Pequêno Poema Infinito*)[41]

It seems that, in the human *imaginaire*, the birth of the *I*[42] is experienced as a violent fragmentation, a mutilation of wholeness, an instance of death.[43] Birth and death are equally present at the moment of origin of the self as an autonomous being. The essence of the tragic is this inextricable association of birth and death, of Eros and Thanatos, which the Pre-Socratics have raised to a meta-physical principle, viz. the convergence of beginnings and ends as we see, e.g., in Anaximander.[44] Mother creates a new being as the result of a double "conception" of life and death. She must conceive, in her unconscious, a "murdered" infant,[45] as well as a living one. If the infant is to develop a psyche, the mother must give it death – in the sense of separation or dis-junction (*sparagmos*) from the maternal fusional unit – so she can give it birth as a separate individual.[46] Neolithic Çatal Hühük statues are striking in their representation of this theme of the inseparable mingling of birth and death: they show women giving birth to animal skulls (see below).

The painful drama of psychic birth as violent fragmentation parallels the double character of physical birth involving an overwhelming mixture of rupture and rapture. It appears that the creation of something alive requires a descent to the depths where the forces of life cohabit with the forces of death. In this primeval world of origins, Eros and Thanatos are not yet differentiated. Mothers at the ecstatic moment of giving birth, or women seized by a "divine madness" descend to a chaotic universe "stirring up the foundations of life from which emanates the odor of death," as Otto puts it rather poetically.[47] We note that *ololygmos* (from the verb *ololyzein*) is an onomatopoeic noun that refers to the cries of women while giving birth. However, the word also refers to the ecstatic shrill of women at the moment of killing the sacrificial animal.[48] In the Odyssey, for example, there is a description of such a sacrifice:

> *Thasymedes, high of heart, came near and dealt the blow; and the axe cut through the sinews of the neck, and loosened the strength of the heifer, and the women raised the sacred cry.*
>
> (ολολυξαν)[49]

Ololygmos is a primitive cry of joy and triumph that bursts out spontaneously at those critical moments of self-transcendence when the forces of life are indistinguishable from the forces of death. It is a cry of both joy and lamentation: *ololygé* also means lament.

Thus, at the root of being, we find the Heraclitean paradoxical coincidence of opposites. Life and death meet in an enigmatic mingling of ecstatic pleasure, abject horror and lamentation. It is ultimately this fundamental enigmatic duality that Dionysos embodies in his two aspects of a life-creating drive and a horrifying agent of death. His erotic mien is a mask that conceals the dreadful countenance of the Lord of the Dead. It is this that makes Dionysos a tragic god and the god of tragedy.

Such a look at Dionysos and his double brings into focus the defining characteristics of tragedy as described by Aristotle. These characteristics involve an unexpected ominous change in the hero's life, fundamental questions of identity, grave misfortunes, mourning, and underlying character "flaws." It is these basic elements that Aristotle considered as essential to tragedy in his treatise on poetry, and we shall have the occasion to return to them. The fundamental, defining structure of tragedy, however, is a radical division of reality that yields two conflicting mutually exclusive positions. This division expresses the tragic duality at the root of being. Division and consequent conflict (αγων) is a *conditio sine qua non* for the birth of the subject; and it is also this same division that casts on the subject the shadow of death, which is at the heart of tragedy.

Notes

1 A.S.Way, *Euripides* (Cambridge, MA: Harvard U. Press, 1979), 3–123.
2 C. Segal, *Dionysiac Poetics and Euripides' "Bacchae"* (Princeton, NJ: Princeton U. Press, 1982).
3 *Ibid.*, 4.
4 G.F. Else, *The Origins and Early Forms of Tragedy* (Cambridge, MA: Harvard U. Press, 1967).
5 Herodotus, *Historiae*, trans. A.D. Godley (Cambridge, MA: Harvard U. Press, 1981), 5.67.
6 Butcher (1951).
7 *Ibid.*, 1449a9–1449a15.
8 Edmonds (1979), 136. Translation by the author.
9 Rohde (1895).
10 Herodotus (1981), 7.111, 2.49.
11 U. von Wilamowitz-Moellendorff, *Der Glaube der Hellenen* (Berlin: Weidmann, 1931).
12 *Ek-stasis* = standing outside oneself.
13 Way (1979), ll. 280–282. Translation by the author.
14 F. Nietzsche, *The Birth of Tragedy from the Spirit of Music*, trans. W. Kaufmann (New York: Random House, 1967).
15 J.E. Harrison, *Themis: A Study of the Social Origins of Greek Religion* (New York: University Books, 1962).
16 See A.W. Pickard-Cambridge, *Dithyramb, Tragedy and Comedy* (Oxford U. Press, 1927).
17 Way (1979), *Bacchae*, 1388–1390. Translation by the author.
18 G.S. Kirk, *The Bacchae by Euripides* (Englewood Cliffs, NJ: Prentice-Hall, 1970), 81.
19 *Ibid.*, 84.
20 *Ibid.*, 117–118.
21 Plato, *Platonis Opera*, ed. J. Burnet (London: Oxford U. Press, 1973), *Phaedrus*, 244a7.
22 Nietzsche (1967), 1087.
23 K.I. Arvanitakis, "Some thoughts on the essence of the tragic," *Int. J. Psycho-Anal.*, 1998: 955–964.
24 G.W.F. Hegel, *The Phenomenology of Mind*, trans. J.B. Baillie (New York: Harper and Row, 1967).
25 Butcher (1951), 1458a26.
26 Herodotus (1981), 2.123.
27 See W. Burkert, *Greek Religion*, trans. J. Raffan (Cambridge, MA: Harvard U. Press, 1985), 237.
28 *Ibid.*, 164.
29 W.F. Otto, *Dionysus, Mythos und Kultus* (Frankfurt: Vittorio Klostermann, 1933).
30 Herodotus (1981), 2.81.
31 Burkert (1985), 293.
32 Otto (1933), 123.
33 Kirk and Raven (1971), 210.
34 *Ibid.*, 211.

35 D.W. Winnicott, *Playing and Reality* (London: Tavistock Publications, 1971).
36 G. Steiner, Absolute Tragedy, in *No Passion Spent* (New Haven: Yale University Press, 1996), 129–141.
37 Slavoj Žižek, *The Parallax View* (Cambridge, MA: MIT Press, 2006).
38 K.I. Arvanitakis, *Psychoanalytic Scholia on the Homeric Epics* (Leiden: Brill, 2015).
39 It was Otto Rank (*The Trauma of Birth*. New York: Dover Publications, 1929) who drew attention to birth trauma and considered it as the foundation of our cultural and individual development.
40 J. Lacan, *Écrits* (Paris: Seuil, 1966).
41 F.G. Lorca, *Selected Poems*, trans. M. Sorrell (New York: Oxford U. Press, 2007), 144.
42 The *I* is used here interchangeably with the self.
43 This may be related to the biological fact – unique to the human species – that the human infant is born prematurely.
44 See Kirk and Raven (1971), 106.
45 S. Leclaire, *On tue un enfant* (Paris: Seuil, 1975).
46 This psychic separation is a distant echo of the first division of the fertilized ovum that will eventually lead to the formation of an embryo. Division is, thus, a necessary condition for the creation of life.
47 Otto (1933), 135.
48 See Burkert (1985), 74.
49 Homer, *The Odyssey*, trans. A.T. Murray (Cambridge, MA: Harvard U. Press, 1995), 3: 448 450.

2 The origin of tragedy

Freud was in his teens when he developed a keen interest in tragedy, and especially in *Oedipus Rex*, as we learn from a letter to his boyhood friend Emil Fluss dated March 17, 1873. As is well known, the story of King Oedipus lay at the heart of Freud's theorizing, especially following the death of his father when oedipal conflicts brought it into focus in his self-analysis (letter to Fliess, October 15, 1897).[1] Freud came to regard the oedipal complex as "the nuclear complex of neurosis."

Over forty years after his first expressed interest in tragedy, Freud turned his attention to a consideration of tragedy's origins. His thinking on that matter was significantly influenced by the then current theories of William Robertson Smith and James Frazer concerning sacrificial ritual meals and the myths related to them. In *Totem and Taboo*, first published in four parts in 1912–1913, Freud advanced his theory that links the origin of tragedy directly to the Oedipus complex.[2] He hypothesized that at the dawn of civilization, a band of men, brothers, came together and killed their father who had been jealously keeping all the females for himself and thus ended the patriarchal horde. Strong ambivalent feelings of triumph and guilt in the sons led to the ritual repetition of the act of parricide, which further strengthened the bond among the clansmen. Freud believed that tragedy emerged from the ritual re-enactment of the ancient murder of the primal father in the forgotten primeval past. Thus, the hero of the tragedy represents the father of the primal horde. It was necessary for him to die because of his "tragic guilt."[3] Freud explained the reason for the hero's guilt by attributing to the sons-chorus a hypocritical "tendentious twist": to exculpate themselves from the guilt of parricide, they projected it into the hero, who now became himself the carrier of the guilt, relieving the chorus from theirs, and thus being responsible for his own demise. Freud interpreted the violent acts and related lamentations of the Dionysian ritual that lay at the root of tragedy in the light of his theory of the murder of the primal father. He was firmly convinced that the oedipal complex is the germinal center from which religion, morals, social organization, as well as all art develop.

In Freud's scheme, this primeval murder has been lost from human memory, but remains alive in the unconscious and is expressed in art and in neurosis. The Oedipus complex transcends the experience of the individual and as a universal unconscious schema is related to "primal phantasy," which Freud believed to be phylogenetically transmitted. The triangulation of the Oedipus complex is, in fact, the central theme of which the various primal phantasies are variants (seduction, primal scene, castration).[4] Parricide could, therefore, be a primal phantasy, a counterpart to castration.

Today, our views regarding primal phantasies have evolved. Freud based his theory of the origin of primal phantasies on Lamarck's belief that acquired traits can be inherited and thus preserved in phylogenesis, and also on Haeckel's theory that ontogenesis recapitulates phylogenesis. However, these theories can no longer be defended. The existence of primal phantasies and their influence in psychic life, however, need not be questioned. It is the manner of their transmission from our remote human past to each individual that is under debate. Such transmission, if not exclusively genetic, can be carried out in combination with cultural factors, effecting a trans-generational conveyance through the maternal unconscious. However, it has also been suggested[5] that primal phantasies may be constructed retroactively in an attempt to answer universal human questions regarding origins, identity, change or order. These fundamental human questions are common to all humanity (explaining the universality of the primal phantasies) because they result from a common genetic makeup that determines our relation to reality (subjective and objective). Thus, we are all born prematurely, we experience and are conscious of one-ness, of two-ness, of triangulation and gaps, we are all exposed to culture, language, symbols etc. From this perspective, Freud's belief in the genetic, biological basis of primal phantasies as expressing mental elaborations of our instinctual life can, therefore, still be maintained. As for the question of ontogenetic repetition of phylogenesis, genetic memory clearly obliterates the distinction between individual (ontogenetic) past and the past of the species (phylogenesis) and keeps a record of the path of evolution.

Regarding the origins of tragedy, the view presented here is a more significant deviation from the Freudian position than the specific mode of transmission of primal phantasies suggested by contemporary studies. It is the very *nature* of the primal event phantasy that is being re-enacted in tragedy. For Freud, this is the original murder of the father by his son(s). We propose, instead, that the primal phantasy enacted in tragedy is a "murder" of the infant by his/her mother.

All primal phantasies, as Laplanche and Pontalis point out,[6] address the enigma of *origins*: the origin of the subject in Freud's "primal scene" (*Ur-szene*), the origin of sexual differences in the primal phantasy of castration, the origin of sexuality in the primal phantasy of seduction. We believe, however, that the primal phantasy addressing the enigma of origins of the subject is not what Freud considered to be the primal scene, viz. the parental intercourse and associated oedipal triangulation, but rather the birth of the subject as the result of a violent rupture of an original fusional undifferentiated oneness-with-mother; a rupture felt as a murder and as death on the level of the imaginary. Time is shrunk at this moment, so the primal scene is also the final scene.[7] Thus, positing the existence of a primal phantasy of a scene of a violent split as the origin of the individual, we suggest that *this* is what is enacted in tragedy and is reflected in the divisions, dualities, contradictions and violent conflicts on multiple levels that characterize tragedy. It is a Dionysian *Ur-szene* of birth and death. Birth, in this phantasy, is experienced as a violent section, a *caesura* of being, and is, therefore, traumatic, leading compulsively to ritualistic repetitions. Hence, tragedy. According to this view, the filicidal act in the *Bacchae* – the tragedy that addresses the very nature of tragedy – is seen as the enactment of a primal phantasy related to the primordial violence of differentiation; the necessary *pathos* that results from the cleavage of the original mother–infant one-ness which creates duality and leads to the birth of the subject as a separate being. This mutilation constitutes the "founding murder,"[8] not the oedipal murder of the father. The focus here shifts to the pre-oedipal and to the maternal. Thus, what is "repeated" in drama is not the oedipal violence as Green[9] maintains, but a more primitive aggression related to mother (*sparagmos*). An "infinite separation" following "infinite unification" is what generates the tragic, as Hölderlin tells us.[10] The tragic hero dies not because of his guilt (Freud), but, in essence, in order to be born (*ov*). At the moment of his death, the hero – or heroine – is born(e) into another level, according to a higher rule of cosmic order (δίκη). From this perspective, Pentheus appears as the prototypical spectator; the spectator of the drama of his origins: he is driven to witness the primordial maternal mysteries (κρυφαιοι χοροι) of enigmatic and contradictory dualities, the maenads' tender succoring of the young fawns and their savage tearing apart of their flesh. Making himself indistinguishable from his mother[11] (the spectator identified with the actor), the disguised Pentheus is the spectator–actor–mutilated victim, torn apart into fragments, re-living in the here-and-now his pre-historic trauma of origins.

Myths are constructed to explain rituals. The Dionysos myth of maternal filicide is a *mise-en-sens*, an etiologic myth of ritual dismemberment, which, in turn, is the ritualistic *mise-en-scène* of a primal phantasy scene of birth as a violent ontologic *caesura*. This is the "real occurrence"[12] in the individual's archaic past that is preserved in the primal phantasy of the tragic. Moreover, in this view, as in the Freudian schema, this primal phantasy is a scenario that resides in the *unconscious*.

Murder, as the core event in Freud's parricidal primal event at the root of tragedy, murder in the filicidal primal phantasy at tragedy's roots according to the present view: in either case, an originary elemental violence that is a fundamental schism is, unquestionably, at the heart of tragedy. This "rent" or division of the very body of tragedy as a genre occurs on multiple levels: historical (cyclic dances/tragedy), structural (episodes/choral parts), "mythic" (humans/gods), linguistic (Attic/Doric dialects), etc. However, death as the primal division is the central theme that brings together all the segmental divisions of the tragic body of this genre. "Human existence face-to-face with death: that is the kernel of τραγῳδια," according to Burkert.[13]

The origin of the fundamental violence embedded in the primal phantasy that gives tragedy its structure must be sought, of course, in the biological instinct that underlies phantasy.[14] Aggression is a biological given[15] which, in the course of human evolution and under the influence of what might be called a *psychic imperative*, becomes mentalized[16] causing phantasies, rituals, thoughts, symbols. It, thus, appears in the phantasy of origins of the individual born as the result of a necessary violent division, of a "deadly" rupture, and it is enacted in a sacrificial ritual of mutilation as a generative act in the service of life. The essence of sacrifice pervades tragedy as tragedy revolves around violence and lamentation. Sacrificial violence touches the roots of human existence, according to Burkert, who maintains that goat-sacrifice "leads us back . . . into the center of tragedy."[17] The formative core of all ritual, he holds, is an encounter with death, and this occurs through a sacrificial killing that guarantees the perpetuation of life through death and provides the ground for civilization. Writing of the emergence of culture, Burkert affirms that "man became man . . . through the act of killing."[18] He explains that "with remarkable consistency myths tell of the origins of man in a fall, a crime that is often a bloody act of violence." These are the myths that provide the mental elaboration of the raw bodily ritual which – according to the present view – is the enactment of a primal phantasy of the birth of the individual as a "bloody act of violence" – this being the phantasy that defines the tragic. However, what Burkert shows is that the origins of *homo sapiens* as a species, as well as the origin of human communities, are also founded on aggression. It is the act of killing that gave birth to human culture. Man as hunter originally hunted other men as well as animals. The hunter identified with his life-giving prey and felt a brotherly bond with it. This generated feelings of guilt and the need to make reparation to the dead prey which took the form of sacrificial rituals that provided forgiveness and reparation, viz. restoring the body's integrity in burial by laying out the bones covered with some flesh and skin, etc. Such rituals created and maintained a communal bond. Killing the prey was another aspect of being alive, as death gives rise to life. The experiential merge of life and death in these early cultures is shown in the Neolithic plaster statues of Çatal Hühük in Anatolia, mentioned above, where some goddesses are found with legs spread apart giving birth to bull or ram skulls. The goddess is the mother of the hunted beasts that are life-giving through their death, "a life-giving power governing the dead," says Burkert.[19] The goddess is a mother, giving life through death and giving death for the sake of life. She is giving birth to death. We regard this as the imago of the archaic Mother in whom life and death are intermingled, the Great Mother Goddess of the primal phantasy of the origin of the individual.

Rituals express the paradoxical inextricable merging of life and death, which makes ritual a "*mysterium tremendum et fascinans*" giving it its character of awe, terror, ecstasy and elation, all at once.[20] The murdered victim is god, the god of life, and this provides the basis of the relation of violence to the sacred. Girard's insightful study is relevant here.[21] Like Burkert, Girard places violence as a biological given at the root of the formation of society and culture. The foundational event, he hypothesizes, was a murder, a spontaneous act of violence (*violence fondatrice*) directed at an emissary victim, carrier of the communal "impurities." This was a cathartic act of expelling destructive forces embedded within the community, allowing that community to re-gain stability. The sacrificed victim thus acquired a dual identity: both as the carrier of destructive violence and as the protector of life and order. This mechanism of expulsion formed the basis of religion and of the sacred. The first murder was forgotten and repeated as a ritual of sacrifice around which the community was united. For Girard, the expulsion and killing of the scapegoat is the key to all ritual. He believes that Greek tragedy arose as an apotropaic ritual that appeared at a time of sacrificial crisis, as the old religious and social order was being replaced by new ideas and values and society was threatened by the risk of decompensating into undifferentiated violence. Tragedy, under the aegis of Dionysos, whom Girard considers as "the god of violence," represented a cathartic foundational violence that aimed to re-establish order. Tragedy was an attempt to revive the sacrificial cult that had lost its power by representing sacrifice symbolically on stage. What we see in the *Bacchae* is the old gods reasserting themselves. The increasing tendency to place man at the center of collective consciousness meant an increasing weakening of the borders between the divine and the human. Established firm distinctions were being obscured, and so tragedy arose out of Dionysian ritual sacrifice in order to re-affirm differentiations, dividing lines, limits and distinctions. The fifth century was, unquestionably, a time of rapid growth and psychosocial maturation, a revolutionary time of increasing awareness that violence is inherent in being and constitutes an inescapable element in the human psyche as well as in society at large ($Aναγκη,\ Moιρα$). It cannot be expelled, purged or foreclosed. It is irreducible and presents itself as the necessary condition for existence; it cannot be resolved away. Tragedy arose, as a consequence, to express the un-resolvability of conflict and contradiction (both inner and outer) and the necessity of the death of the hero if he is to claim "true" existence, if meta-physical balance is to be preserved. The hero *must* die: no other outcome is possible. In the emerging new era, a compelling "Either/Or" coexisted with an irreducible *equilibrium* of opposing forces (Hölderlin's *Gleichgewicht*). The hero, being the carrier of archaic destructive forces (Titanic?[22]), is condemned to exist by falling and to carry a bodily knowledge of the incomprehensible inevitability of his destiny. In the words of George Steiner,[23] "[the hero] strides to his fierce disaster in the grip of truths more intense than knowledge."

Girard, like Burkert, focuses his interest on the vital role of aggression in the birth of community and social organization, not in intra-individual dynamics. However, the birth of the individual *I* is – we hold – preserved in phantasy as the result of an act of violence. Girard's "first murder" or expulsion, under the mechanism of projecting out the evil as a means of catharsis, presupposes the existence of a concept of evil which must come before the designation of the first emissary victim. The act of expulsion is based on a concept which is an echo of the primal phantasy of a *violent expulsion of the self*, a mentalized traumatic act that is now to be mimetically repeated in an active mode, with the scapegoat as the passive victim. Thus, the sacrificial ritual re-enacts the original expulsion of the self, a bodily schism that had been suffered passively by the individual. The key to all ritual, therefore, is not the expulsion/killing of the emissary victim, as Girard proposes, but rather what lies behind it, namely the phantasy of the expulsion/killing of the self at the time of differentiation/separation-rupture of the original fused One (motherinfant). The birth of the individual, if viewed from the perspective of the mechanism of the *bouc émissaire*, would take on the character of a "cathartic" event attributing to the individual an immanent violence, a hybristic cosmic stain to be purged "according to necessity" by its sacrificial expulsion/death-birth in order to re-establish cosmic order and justice. Specifically, the retribution required as atonement for the "existential guilt" borne by the individual necessitates a co-incidence of beginning and end, of birth and death: this seems to be the import of Anaximander's famous fragment called "the first statement of Western thought":

> *The same* [elements] *constitute the birth of beings and their decomposition, according to necessity* [κατα το χρεων]. *For they give each other justice and penalty for injustice* [αδικια], *according to the order of time.*[24]

In conclusion, both the birth of human society, and the birth of the individual as an *I* conscious of itself, are indissociably linked with violence and death. Ostensibly the dynamics of the process that led to the emergence of organized communities repeat the dynamics of the process that led to the emergence of the *I*. This dynamic provides the ground for the emergence of tragedy.

If we view the putative specifics of Aristotle's account of the origin of tragedy from the viewpoint adopted here, it would seem that the primal phantasy of the birth of the individual as the result of a deadly rupture of an original "whole" is reflected in the very manner in which tragedy itself was born, as well as in the various divisions on multiple levels evident within the body (form) of tragedy mentioned above. It is as if the primal scene cast its shadow on the process that led to the emergence of tragedy, as well as on its structure, so that the aesthetic of tragedy is grounded on the ontology of the individual. However, first, some preliminary remarks. Aristotle defined tragedy as the *mimesis* of a momentous act.[25] This act, he specified, is of the order of things that *might* happen (οια αν γενοιτο[26]), i.e., not historical events. Therefore, the act belongs to the realm of fantasy. We posit here that behind the various fantasy scenes that tragedy imitates there is, ultimately, the fantasy that relates to the very identity of the hero, the (unconscious) *p*hantasy of the *Ur-szene* of the birth of the individual. It is the imitation of that act that will bring about the recognition of "who is what."[27] The scene we witness on stage is, therefore, twice removed from the original act, and is the imitation of an imitation, insofar as Aristotle's fantasy act is a sort of imitation of a primal phantasy act. To complicate things even further, the original phantasy itself can be said to be a sort of imitation of a pre-verbal, pre-mental, archaic *bodily* act lacking visual representability, of which it is the mentalization (through a process of "figurability"[28]). Phantasy here records a memory without content, an event that lies outside memory. Aristotle considered *mimesis* as "innate" (συμφυτον) in humans and as a means of learning. The imitation of a mental act on stage points to what has been regarded as being characteristic of Greek culture, namely that it was a culture of the eyes, a visual culture, and, under these conditions, imitation constitutes a "learning" activity according to Aristotle. However, significantly, once a phantasy/fantasy act is imitated, i.e., reproduced on stage, the issue of *duality* is already irrevocably posited. The duality/division, which is the theme of the phantasy, is now enacted via mimetic doubling in the very process of the birth of tragedy.

Looking now at this process more closely, we can visualize how and at which point in the process the "division theme" of the primal scene was "repeated" or enacted, giving birth and shape to the new genre that appeared in fifth century Athens. We hypothesize that it all started with an agitated circular group ritual dance around a tomb or altar, either of a dead hero (Adrastos?), or of a sacrificed god (Dionysos) – let this remain unspecified – but, in either case, we posit a circular dance centered around death. The "chorus" was engaged in a lament, supplication and/or awe and sacred terror. Maybe ritual lament choruses around the tomb of a hero existed before the arrival of Dionysos to Greek soil. Herodotos[29] tells us that it was Cleisthenes of Sikyon, early in the sixth century BCE, who transferred to Dionysos the "tragic choruses" that had been, until then, performed in lamenting ceremonies for the death Adrastos, the local hero. Yet, there were Dionysian dithyramb composers (Arion), and *tragodoi* singers already in the seventh century BCE. However, whether the circular dances were originally Dionysian or secondarily attributed to Dionysos and merged with his Phrygian dithyramb is of little import to our argument. The important question is the possibility that the original circular *tragoikoi choroi* were in relation to death, lamentation and supplication, a fact that would explain the centrality of death in tragedy. The crucial moment occurred, as Aristotle testifies, when, in a spontaneous act of "improvisation," a member of the circular ritual group *broke off*, differentiating himself from the round mass, thereby becoming the first actor, and introducing language and dialogue. This is believed to have been the innovation of Thespis in 535 BCE, the actor and poet (who had composed a *Pentheus*) who is also said to have introduced the mask. So, now, we have the division of the undifferentiated original "whole" (the group of ritual worshippers) into two parts (chorus and actor), and we also have the division within the individual dancer who assumes *another* identity personified by the mask. The duality, i.e., the splitting that occurs in the phantasy primal scene of the birth of the individual, is repeated here, re-doubled in the process of the birth of tragedy (as it had, also, been re-doubled in the birth of organized communities through the expulsion of the scapegoat). The chorus leader, the *exarchos* (cf. θρηνων εξαρχος, "the leader of the mourners" in *Iliad*[30]), separates himself from the circle and becomes the protagonist of a tragedy. Language and the symbolic function are now irrevocably introduced and bind the hero via dialogue with the body of the chorus – with the physicality of that gyrating chanting mass. The dialogue itself, i.e., language, becomes a carrier of the tragic as it now names a *gap*, an object lost. The structure of tragedy that results from all this displays a division between the choral parts and the episodes (reflecting the division between the original chorus and the leader), accompanied by a linguistic split evident in the Doric dialect characteristic of the chorus, contrasting with the Attic dialect of the actors.

The chain of divisions and splits within the structure of tragedy, however, doesn't stop here. As the actor appears – a masked double of himself – an audience appears, separated from the space of the ritual and assuming the role of spectator, observing from the side. There is now the space for the actors and a separate space for the spectators. The oldest Greek theater at Thorikos (late sixth century BCE) reflects this arrangement: unlike the curved amphitheaters of later times, the Thorikos theater consists of a semi-elliptical elongated row of seats on one side of the orchestra. The intriguing feature of this theater is its location, which is in physical contiguity to a cemetery. A pre-historic cemetery existed there from Mycenaean times, but, just south of the orchestra, a later cemetery was found which dates possibly from the time that the theater itself was constructed in historical times. This would follow the thesis of an intimate relation between early Greek theater and ritual lamentation that Ridgeway has proposed.[31]

Interestingly, the architectural design of the amphitheater of classical and Hellenistic times *itself* might be said to reflect and be a reminder of the determining primal scene of amputation: it is as if the missing part of the inverted cone – the space now occupied by the *skene* – represents the wound left by the original rupture of the round body of the archaic chorus. That circular body was, in a manner of speaking, the primal womb bursting with creative energy, which ruptured to give birth to the hero. Its circularity manifests the body's cyclic rhythms, a continuous repetition of regularly recurring body events that provide the basis of fantasies of "eternal returns," of changelessness and immortality. When the sphere was sundered, split open expelling a fragment (the hero), the continuity of the circle/cycle was broken, interrupting the flow of circular time and giving birth to linear time, to irreversible loss and mourning, to the tragic. The "segmented" or amputated amphitheater – its very architecture representing the tragic – thus made its appearance as a life space.

With the hero thrust out of the circular mass, a curious dynamic develops between hero and chorus. The hero now occupies a position "off-center" – Aristotle would call it a *hamartia*. However, the hero is, now, what is called in medicine a *hamartoma*: a hybristic monster. The chorus views him as a foreign body, a blasphemous rebel that caused a breach in the original fusional harmony of the choral mass, opening up an irremediable wound in its body. Yet, simultaneously, the chorus members are in awe of the hero; the hero who is now *autonomos, autognotos*.[32] The chorus both repudiates the hero's actions, attempting to seduce him back into the established order (traditional rational wisdom) but, at the same time, pushes him further into the chaos that engulfs the lone actor (*monê*) who dares to challenge the Eternal Laws. The chorus members both disengage from and disown the hero, but also exploit him by projecting into him their own forbidden wild wishes and assigning to him the task of acting them out. Thus, the chorus, which was originally the space of Dionysian madness, gradually becomes an agency of reason, having projected all its irrationality into the split-off hero.[33] The hero as the *scapegoat* has betrayed and is betrayed by the chorus, but is also the incarnation of the chorus' mad wishes.

Moreover, the hero-goat will be both sacrificed and glorified. In assuming such contradictory attitudes, the chorus changes the course of the action, a change mirrored and shared by the "chorus" of spectators (*katharsis*). The chorus' *katharsis* is brought about by the split-off *exarchos*/hero carrying off with him (as the *pharmakos* did) the chorus' primitive madness, while the spectators are equally relieved by the fall of their double.

In the end, the confrontation between the One and the Many designates the conflict (*αγων*) between the unruly, "flawed," hybristic body and the rational mind, or between the divine and the human. The hero is "off the mark" insofar as he is located at the other side of a gap – he *is* a gap – and his body carries the memory of destructive/creative forces of his originary fragmentation. As in the primal horde, the hero is born as an excrescence/excrement/*bouc émissaire* so that the chorus/spectators can be purged. He is doomed to be a sacrificed hero/god. In a more precise manner, however, the hero is "flawed" because in his hybristic autonomy and yearn for the Ideal (a return to the original One) he ignores the *limits* and limitations imposed on humans by the "immortal gods," and, in that sense, he is ignorant of his true identity. His own *anagnorisis* (recognition of true identity) is intrinsically linked with a tragic *peripeteia* (reversal of his situation), *pathos* (suffering) and the *threnos* (mourning) associated with it.[34] The hero's double *hamartia* of both being off-center and ignoring it will lead to his demise. This is tragic insofar as his death is the condition of his existence.

The fundamental division that structures tragedy (ultimately, the division between the mortal hero defined by limits and unlimited divinity) is the final visual manifestation of the primal phantasy of the birth of the individual as a fragment that was violently broken off from a Whole of perfection; a birth marked by death, a separation, an amputation or dislocation that the *I* will always carry as a body memory of its own death and will forever strive to reverse.

The invisible specter of death (always off-stage) is the indisputable Master in tragedy. To repeat Burkert's aphorism, the kernel of tragedy is human existence face-to-face with death. Pickard-Cambridge stressed that the experience of the dead as a living force is intrinsic to tragedy.[35] Death intermingled with life: this is the *Ur-szene* of tragedy.

The frequently debated question of whether tragedy as a genre is possible today is meaningful only if what we have in mind is the specific art form that was crafted by the classical Greek poets. The tragic that breathes through tragedy manifesting the primal phantasy of origins, however, is independent of a given literary form and, as the human condition, has not changed since Classical Antiquity. It will require a genetic mutation of *homo sapiens* to change that, something that hasn't happened yet. The tragic remains for humans an existential law.[36] For Scheler, it is "an essential element of the universe" and "a specific feature of the world's makeup."[37] The tragic is expressed today by Ibsen, Strindberg, O'Neill, Beckett, Müller et al. and in many forms. It pivots – as it always has – on loss and mourning, defiance and defeat, toleration and revolt. The incomprehensible merge of irreconcilables (Eros is Thanatos), the unyielding force of binding Necessity that rules over inescapable double binds and irreducible conflicts provide for modern man, no less than for the classical Greek, a sort of negative concavity within which meaning is generated and undone. The lucidly "obscure" Herakleitos insisted: Being converges towards itself by diverging from itself.

Notes

1 See S. Freud, *La naissance de la psychanalyse*, trans. A. Berman (Paris: PUF., 1969), 196.
2 Freud, *S.E.* 13: 155–161.
3 Freud, here, adopted the German mistranslation of Aristotle's *hamartia* as *Schuld*, "guilt" in the Biblical sense, rather than "error," "error in judgement," as was intended by Aristotle.
4 J. Laplanche and J-B Pontalis, *Vocabulaire de la psychanalyse* (Paris: PUF., 1976), 83.
5 R. Perron, "The unconscious and primal phantasies," *Int. J. Psycho-Anal.*, 2001: 583–595.
6 J. Laplanche and J-B. Pontalis, "Fantasme originaire, fantasmes des origines, origine du fanatasme," *Les Temps Modernes*, 1964: 1833–1868.
7 K.I. Arvanitakis, "An update on time," *Int. J. Psycho-Anal.*, 2005: 531–534.
8 For more classical views of the "foundational murder" see B. Chervet, *Le meurtre fondateur* (Paris: PUF, 2015).

9 A. Green, *Un oeil en trop* (Paris: Les Éditions de Minuit, 1969). See, also, M. Ellman, *Psychoanalytic Literary Criticism* (London: Longman, 1994).

10 F. Hölderlin, "On Tragedy: 'Notes on Oedipus'," *Comparative Criticism*, 1983: 203.

11 "looking at you it is [her] that I see," Dionysos exclaims.

12 Freud, *S.E.* 16: 371.

13 W. Burkert, "Greek tragedy and sacrificial ritual," *Greek Roman and Byzantine Studies*, 1966: 87–121.

14 Isaacs (1948).

15 K. Lorenz, *On Aggression* (Toronto: Bantam, 1967).

16 Bion's alpha-function describes the process of the mentalization of raw sensory data so that they can be thought. W. Bion, *Second Thoughts* (London: Karnac, 1984).

17 Burkert (1966), 121.

18 W. Burkert, *Homo Necans*, trans. P. Bing (Berkeley: U. of California Press, 1983), 22.

19 *Ibid.*, 79.

20 R. Otto, *Le Sacré* (Paris: Payot, 1995).

21 R. Girard, *La violence et le sacré* (Paris: Grasset, 1972).

22 Man carries the ancestral guilt of his origin from the ashes of the Titans who were thunderbolted by Zeus for having torn to pieces his son Dionysos (*Orphic Hymn* 37.4).

23 G. Steiner, *The Death of Tragedy* (New Haven: Yale U. Press, 1961), 7.

24 Kirk and Raven (1971), 106. Translation by the author.

25 Butcher (1951), 1449b24.

26 *Ibid.*, 1451a38.

27 *Ibid.*, 1448b15–b17.

28 C. Botella and S. Botella, "Psychic figurability and unrepresented states," in *Unrepresented States and the Construction of Meaning*, eds. H. Levine, W. Reed and D. Scarfone (London: Karnac, 2013).

29 Herodotus (1981), 5.67.

30 Homer (1920), *Iliad*, XXIV: 721.

31 W. Ridgeway, *The Origin of Tragedy* (New York: Benjamin Blom, 1966).

32 Sophocles, *Antigone*, trans. F. Storr (Cambridge, MA: Harvard U. Press, 1981), l. 821.

33 Regarding this gradual transformation of the chorus, we can clearly observe an evolution from the more "bodily" chorus of the *Choephoroi* to the more mental/rational chorus of *Antigone* and *Philoktetes*. The chorus of the *Bacchae* represents Euripides' revolutionary retrogression to the "bodily" chorus.

34 Butcher (1951), 1452a22–1453a12.

35 Pickard-Cambridge (1927), 106–107.

36 M. Storm, *After Dionysus* (Ithaka: Cornell U. Press, 1998), 70.

37 M. Scheler, "On the Tragic," *Cross Currents*, 1954: 178–191.

3 The origin of theater

The following story was told to me by an Italian friend, a neuroscientist. He was attending a conference in Portugal. That afternoon, after a busy day's sessions, he was walking around with some colleagues, visiting the exciting sights of the charming ancient town where the meeting had been taking place. The group suddenly came upon a chapel that was constructed by using human bones, skulls, femurs, tibias, etc. as building materials. They were all startled, stared motionless for a moment, and then, spontaneously, some of the Italians started an animated street act, a Neapolitan *sceneggiata*, mimicking the imaginary builders of the chapel. It was a pantomime with improvised dialogue and exaggerated gestures, expressing mixed feelings of feigned grief, mockery and laughter but also puzzlement and hints of underlying fear and horror. The comic element side by side with tragic awe. As if, in front of something alien and incomprehensible, yet uncannily familiar, the "actors" resorted to a spontaneous and uncontrolled act whose intention was to both own up to their deep affinity to the "object" in front of them and repudiate it simultaneously. As if at first frozen into immobility by identifying with the dead parts in front of them, they compulsively began a feverish act of revitalizing them. Is this the "magic" power of theater? Lacoue-Labarthe[1] aptly points out: "It is this, perhaps, that constitutes the Tragic: the 'consciousness' or rather – which is the same – the *avowal* that all one can do with death is to theatricalize it." One might ask "is this an act of doubling it in order to undo it?"

The question we wish to raise here is whether *all* theater, not only tragedy, finds its roots in a body memory of a violent primordial ontological schism that is lived, experienced and encoded in body memory as "death," and whether, therefore, all theater is fundamentally tragic. Whether the theatrical act is the final stage of a series of mimetic repetitions with their starting point in the body's inherent aggressive energy, or "division principle" ("Thanatos"), which, in the course of psychological development, is mentalized as an unconscious phantasy of a violent primal scene, which is then repeated in a ritual and is, finally, re- re-re-presented on the "illusory" ludic space of the theater. Such multiple compulsive repetitions (Freud) would point to the severely traumatic nature of the original splitting event. The view that an unconscious memory of a primordial scission at the bodily core of the self (ego)[2] lies at the origin of the theatrical setting and the theatrical act is suggested by the very structure of theater – its defining characteristic – viz. the onto-logical split between the *I*-spectator and the *I*-actor. It would appear that theater's structural split, embodying two registers of reality, "re-calls" the original violent rupture by repeating it. From this viewpoint, the sight of death at the Chapel of Bones at Évora gets linked up, at the speed of light (or rather of darkness), with the primeval moment of a bodily, pre-conceptual state of existential fracture equated with annihilation. This is the moment of what will, later, be narrated to the self as a primal loss, the loss of one's integrity, the mythic loss of One-ness,[3] an ontological loss: the meaning of Death. In the theatrical act triggered by the sight of the mass of bones, the unconscious memory of a trauma that cannot be remembered because it lacks representability is made present, demand-ing urgently to be represented. However, if it is to be represented, it must be subjected to a repetition of violence to make it figurable, first to the mind (phantasy) and then back to the body (theater). This repeated violence resides in the fact that the compulsory transfer (*meta-phor*) of the original traumatic body state to a primal phantasy (i.e., its mentalization) is a categorical leap, a qualitative transmutation – a "translation" – which constitutes an act of violence and betrays the original in the act of "framing" it. The original will be betrayed again by *disguising* it in the *sceneggiata*. The betrayal will continue by the re-telling of the story by my friend, right down to my own recounting it here. The self-multiplying mirror images, far from attenuating the primal trauma, render it a pow-erful vehicle of life instead. Freud believed that the active repetition of what had been suffered passively as trauma aims at "mastering" the trauma. Rather than an ego strategy to "tame" a destructive force, the evolution of trauma through its endless repetitions may be better under-stood as its erotic creative transformation that turns it into a force in the service of life.

Accordingly, we venture to propose that, not only in tragedy but in theater in general, we re-enact the story of our origins as individu-als in a primordial "Big Bang," in a creative eruption that marked the beginning of the history of the *I* as a divided and amputated entity. We propose, in other words, that the tragic duality of Dionysos is embed-ded in *all* theater, that all theater is essentially Dionysian and, hence, tragic, operating under the sign of Dionysos, Lord of the Underworld. Theater has its roots in rituals of mythic generative violence that enact the original trauma of division and consequent duality.[4] The defining character of theater's binary structure, anchored on the primal body and manifested in theater's structural divisions on several levels, reflects – and is explained by – the primal ontological rupture. The tragic as an *a priori* in human matters provides the meta-theatrical or rather pre-theatrical infrastructure of all theater.

Blau's thought intricately develops the division theme stressing that the foundation of theater is fracture and separation. "The condition of theater is an *initiatory breach* which remembers the primal violence," he says.[5] Schechner[6] examines the specific avenues that the ontological division follows in order to make itself manifest. He believes that the specific source of what is performed is to be found in dreams, arguing that, together with bipedal posture, brain size, etc., a chief characteristic of *homo sapiens* that emerged in his evolution is his need to perform his dreams. These "enacted" dreams are the translation of dreams into "doable acts of the body." Dreams, however – we must add – have a long psychic pre-history that goes far back through phantasies to a primordial formless pre-mental body state; the performed "doable acts" of theater, we propose, are the distant and distorted echo of that state. It is the body of this primordial state that was the actor and the acted upon, all at once, in the original eruption that constituted the primal scene. In the process that led to theater, linear time, as well as spatial extension, were shrunk condensing everything to the magnetic "here-and-now" of the doable body acts of performance.

The irresistible question: why this *need*? Before any possible "therapeutic" value that we might invoke to explain such performances, it would seem that it is the absolute and rigid conservatism of the instincts – both of the life and the death instinct – that is at play here. This is a *compulsion*, rather than a need. It is as if instincts are destined to operate within a closed circle, "eternally returning" to their point of departure, in conformity with Anaximander's dictum. This shows theater to be a play of life and of death, the two condensed into one.

Following Schechner, or moving one step back, it would be more accurate to say that in theater, rather than dreams, we perform our unconscious *phantasies:* phantasies that attempt to provide answers to our insistent questions of origins, and – first and foremost – to the question of our own origin as an individual *I*. Phantasies are a peculiar product of our evolution as species. What makes them peculiar is their bi-morphous nature, being both mental and somatic, bridging over the categorical gap by occupying a fertile intermediary space.[7] Phantasies are the carriers of a contradiction, embodying, ultimately, the contradiction of being. The biological origin of this contradiction can be attributed to the "rebellious" runaway growth of the human brain, leaving the rest of the body behind, as it were. The asymmetrical, disharmonious, "neoplastic" growth of the brain generates phantasies, mental products which, however, retain their roots in the body. It is, ultimately, our mind's bonds to the body that explain our epistemic restraints and limitations, such as our incapacity to conceive of anything in a fashion other than binary: the *a priori* of duality. The universal themes addressed by the primal phantasies mentioned earlier (Chapter 2) result from the brain's dissonance with the body, and as such, they represent foci of traumata. It would seem that phantasies are attempts by the organism to deal with these. Such foci are related to the fundamental questions concerning origins and ends, identity, multiple realities, loss, meaning, relations, etc. The number of universal primal phantasies genetically inscribed in the unconscious is, therefore, limited. They become manifest by taking a sensible (principally visual) form and being expressed via an infinite number of "scenaria" that can be enacted in fantasy (conscious), in dream, in psychopathology (neuroses, psychoses, psychosomatoses), in ritual, in culture and in art. Among the various primal phantasies, a central place is accorded to the phantasy that relates to the origin of the individual and regards its birth as the result of a primal trauma. Theater would seem to occupy a special position among the arts in the enactment of this "primal scene" because it is the only art form that re-presents it directly in its *original medium*: the body – rather than in sound, canvas, stone, language or thought. Moreover, it must be added that, in bringing the primal trauma explicitly back to the body, theater is by its very method, a violent act.

And yet, we take pleasure in theater – although this is a peculiar kind of "pleasure." The ambiguity of such pleasure is related to that indefinable paradoxical state of the Winnicottian "good enough mother" with her baby, in their first few months together and apart. This mother–infant "dual unit" – two yet one – navigating between ecstasy and disaster, illusion and disillusion, is the quintessence of the Dionysian state, divided yet fused, erotic and thanatic all at once, an intermediary state located in the *in-between* of life and death: the Dionysian space of theater. The theatrical moment is indeed psychically archaic.

The proposed model of the sequence of events that led to the emergence of theater attempts to conceptualize the origins of this seemingly strange and uncanny human activity based on insights gained from psychoanalysis and is admittedly – perhaps unavoidably – biased. We hold that there is a specifically human need, a compulsion, to imitate "reality," to duplicate it and to undo it at the same time. The driving force behind this activity – we surmise – is an archaic trauma. The traumatic nature of this event is at the core of a fundamental ambiguity that resides in our sense of *I* and our experience of reality. The ineradicable question plaguing humans is an incessant: "Which *I?*" and "Which reality?"[8] Fragmentation and polymorphy are both given. Herein lies the nature of the trauma, and the reason Freud considered the *Todestrieb* primary and older than Eros.

The roots of the "death drive" are to be found in the biological instinct of aggression. Man's challenge is to develop the means of converting part of that destructive energy into life-sustaining activities. The first use of pebble tools may have been to kill a rival, and the first vestiges of regular fire use have been found side by side with mutilated and roasted human remains. Yet, in time, man began to bury his dead, developed elaborate funeral rituals and discovered himself in his cave drawings. Lorenz[9] speaks of this enigmatic Janus creature, divided within a unit: animal and symbol, all in one. *Ecce homo.*

The mysterious transformation of biological energy into a mental force in *homo sapiens* has, unquestionably, survival value. This "transfer" from the body to the mind, which could be called the *primal meta-phor*, is what gives rise to phantasies as somato-mental events. Phantasies are our proto-thoughts. The phantasy of our origins in an ambiguous act of birth and death, our *Ur-szene*, articulates a traumatic pre-symbolic experience of loss and irreversibly posits the fundamental duality of presence–absence on which the *I–You* distinction (our identity) is founded. The *I* is born dislocated, carrying the *hamartia* of its ontological amputation. Human reality (both inner and outer) is, accordingly, divided *a priori*.

In the life of the infant, the sense of loss of the primal One-ness is concretized during moments of a mother's absence. Such moments represent the *realization*, or materialization of the traumatic primal phantasy and can be catastrophic if prolonged. The experience is formless, incomprehensible and is "felt"[10] – we assume – as a total existential collapse since it occurs before the emergence of a thinking apparatus and a differentiated body-mind system. The fear of annihilation, of death, is present in the Unconscious according to Klein who disagreed with Freud on this issue. Bion[11] described such states of collapse as occurring, also, when the infant's fear of annihilation fails to be modified by what he calls mother's "reverie." Mother's reverie is her receptive capacity to take onto and into herself such fears of disintegration, process them psychically, give them meaning and communicate them back to her infant in a liveable form. When this does not happen, the infant is thrown into a state of "nameless dread." Psychotic states later on, feelings of being dead and distressful states of meaninglessness originate here. Moments of such collapse in infancy call for urgent measures to re-create the lost object (the lost state). Theater can be said to have its roots in attempts to re-capture the lost object-self. It does so in a paradoxical and contradictory manner: by creating a double of the lost object (self), and by positing *ipso facto* an ontological gap that the spectator is called upon to bridge. Theater arose as an attempt to deal with the incomprehensible void felt to be at the heart of being. Thus, the motives and the specific nature of the theatrical act can be traced to the earliest moments of loss of being related to mother's absence in infancy that was indistinguishable from a catastrophic loss of the *self*, and to the maneuvers resorted to in order to deal with it.

There is an illuminating observation by Freud[12] casually witnessing a scene involving his one-and-a-half year grandson that is of relevance here. This is the famous *Fort-da* game which has been extensively studied and analyzed from diverse perspectives and regarded as the basis of several significant achievements of psychological growth. The little boy is playing with a wooden reel attached to a string. He holds the reel by the string and skillfully throws it over the edge of his curtained[13] cot, so it disappears as he utters an expressive "o-o-o-o" ("fort" = "gone"). He then pulls the string again until the reel appears from behind the cot's curtain and exclaims a joyful "da" ("there"). One way of understanding what is going on is to say that the little boy had found a way of dealing with his mother's absence (to whom, we are told, he was "greatly attached") by staging this short play in which the object is lost, but is then, through the child's own action, made to reappear from behind the curtain. What is even more significant, however, is the frequently neglected footnote to the description of this game. Parallel to his staging mother's disappearance and her return, the little boy, Freud tells us in the footnote, staged his own disappearance and re-appearance:

> During [a] *long period of solitude the child had found a method of making himself disappear. He had discovered his reflection in a full-sized mirror which did not quite reach to the ground, so that by crouching down he could make his mirror-image "gone."*

Here, little Ernst is having a visual dialogue with his double, his absent self. Freud considered this child's capacity to deal with loss and absence through the "staging" of a play (the loss involving not only the object but, concurrently, the self as well) as a "great cultural achievement." Can we not consider this elemental drama as the primal moment and foundation of theater? The one-and-a-half-year-old child's play act to deal with the lost object had been preceded by an earlier, imagined "play" in infancy, when the absent object could be made present on a mental stage only, via a hallucination ("hallucinatory fulfillment"). Now, however, the child has gone a step further by utilizing external reality and introducing there the presence of his absent self. The absent body, Lacan's "mutilated body" (*corps morcelé*),[14] reconstitutes itself as a *revenant*, a ghost that returns. However, the body that re-appears, the double, the specular self, is an immaterial body, a thought that has incorporated absence and is always both "here and elsewhere." It is an *ek-static* dislocated presence, a subject *of* absence and subject *to* absence, subject to death. It is Heidegger's *Platzhalter des Nichts*,[15] and Artaud's "sign."[16] It is the Actor.

The early traumatic states of the loss of the object recur in certain situations in later life, situations that do not involve actual (current) loss, as psychoanalysis has shown. We can speculate (specular projection is, here, our only epistemic tool) that in humanity's remote past, at some point in the course of our evolution, the experience of primeval man in front of a dead body awakened in his deep unconscious[17] the earliest body state of annihilation; a state of deadness and of nameless dread, alternating with states of disorientation and bewilderment that had followed the sudden loss of the primary object and the perception of the not-me reality as an estranged, alienated self. This – we imagine – was a moment of unspeakable terror, particularly since it was mixed with a strange attraction. It is likely that in early societies it led – as in the case of the group of neuroscientists at the bone Chapel of Évora – to a ritual act activated by the unconscious phantasy of primal alienation at birth. Violence, dismemberment, disintegration, annihilation are the defining features of this phantasy, and these would be the key elements of the ritual which may have been the beginning of theater. The breakdown, dis-order, dis-organization and estrangement characteristic of the situation came to signify madness and death, and these states constituted the underlying psychological atmosphere of theater. The Great Other ruled the scene: Dionysos. The ghost of the self that now re-appears, mad and alien yet deeply familiar, is the actor Dionysos, the liminal god between the visible and the invisible, between madness and sanity, between the living and the dead. Dionysos' dual function as the god of theater and god of the dead underlines the intrinsic connection between theater and death.[18]

Recent decades have shown a renewed interest in the ritual nature of theater. The insistence on ritual as the core of the theatrical act goes back to the prophetic visions of Artaud in the 1930s that left an indelible mark on modern theater. Grotowski,[19] in the tradition of Appia, Craig and Meyerhold, sought to restore the original ritual purity of theater (the "primal ritual") by creating a "modern secular ritual." Schechner, in several publications and productions in the 1960s became the principal proponent of the ritual thesis.[20] However, before Schechner, a significant development in this direction had appeared in Germany at the turn of the nineteenth century which was to have its full fruition a couple of generations later in the so-called "post-dramatic" theater that characterizes much of the theater of our days.[21] This was the "performative turn" that was initiated by Max Herrmann which brought about a shift from myth/text to the actor's real body.[22] The theatrical event was no longer the enactment of a story for an observer-spectator located on the other side of a curtain, but a *performance* that abolished the boundaries between actor and spectator bringing them together in a shared (communal) physical bodily experience (on a physiological as well as on an emotional level), an experience that was transformative. Post-dramatic theater since the 1970s is no longer axed on the text; it is anti-text and anti-theatrical illusion.[23] The action space has moved from the mind to the body, from the symbolic to the pre-symbolic and from the individual to the shared communal. This is most clearly seen in the work of Terzopoulos who advocates a "return to the Dionysian body" and has developed a "biodynamic" method that aids the actor to achieve this.[24] Performance theater of this kind recaptures the characteristics of a ritual. It is a return to proto-theater of the primitive chorus. In our contemporary "society of spectacle," post-dramatic theater seeks to disturb our collective lethargy, our passive receptivity of socially fabricated "simulacra" by a shocking presentation of a different, an inner *archaic* space and time (lived time, Bergson's *durée*). Such recent developments in theater could be seen as healing maneuvers undertaken by the traumatized postmodern subject, painfully conscious of its inner structural fissures and gaps, and seeking to "re-work," so to speak, its trauma of origins, the trauma inscribed in a bodily primal phantasy of ontological split. We, thus, seem, in our contemporary theater, to be re-visiting the primal phantasy and the ritual related to it. Theater is now closer to the body, closer to the primal trauma (pre-mental), closer to a wound that refuses to heal. Unquestionably, these developments result from complex sociocultural changes. However, we must ask: to what extent has psychoanalysis contributed to this turn towards the "archaic," the "primitive," towards the body as the un-mediated expression of what language conceals? I believe that psychoanalysis – specifically post-Freudian psychoanalysis – has, indeed, played a significant role. It has led to the awareness that the text, the plot, is a shield, a defense against deeper layers of a disorganizing pre-symbolic trauma. The text is what *resists* the theatrical act.

Schechner speaks of performance as being "exteriorized fantasy." The theory that fantasy provides the substance of theater has, also, been proposed by Rozik.[25] Rozik's thesis is that the roots of theater are pre-linguistic mental images which, for purposes of communication, are imprinted on the concrete medium of the human body. These mental images find concrete expression and are at the root of other art media as well (visual, musical, literary), as they are, also, at the root of pre-historic rock paintings, mimetic dances and rituals, but these are all independent of each other. In particular, Rozik argues that there is no convincing evidence that ritual is the precursor of theater as has been claimed. These views accord with the views presented here. We may allow that ritual needn't be a necessary intermediary between the primal phantasy and theater. Rozik, however, doesn't single out the *unconscious phantasy of a primal schism* as the one mental image – the mental image *par excellence* – that alone lies at the root of theater as proposed here. In the bodily enactment of this phantasy, the archaic pre-mental bodily state of origins buried in the deepest layers of the Unconscious is accessed, and this is the state of Artaud's actor "signaling through flames," or of Grotowski's actor "discovering his ancient corporality."

Theater is not the visible figuration of the Unconscious as fantasies and dreams are, it is not a fantasy acted out, or a dream-in-flesh, but neither is it the "in-carnation" of an infinite number of unconscious phantasy scenaria. We suggest that it is the incarnated re-enactment of *a specific* unconscious trauma, an archaic trauma located in the pre-ver-bal "physical" regions of the psyche, in the pre-symbolic. The actor, however, does not merely re-present something (the archaic body state); he/she aims to present the pre-mental scenario of the Incomprehensible and is, ultimately, the "representative" of the un-representable. The space of theater is, thus, the space of the psychotic, the space into which the fragmented self's alienated dead parts, its "bizarre objects"[26] are pro-jected. Hence all theater is theater of death. The relationship between theater and death is, according to this view, organic.

What emerges from all this is a certain conceptual "architectural plan" of theater. It consists of two symmetrical universes, mirror images of each other (*I*-actor, *I*-spectator), collapsing into each other and dueling with each other. Each comprises three areas, of three spaces. First, the stage. Behind it, and communicating with it through a "door of magic," the backstage. Finally, a third space that cannot be located – let's say it is "somewhere" – which we can call the space "O" (without specifying whether this is the letter O of origin, or the figure zero). Visible events are taking place on the stage. The mysterious backstage is the space where the phantasy of the primal scene resides – a scene of death and of generation at once – that will enter through the door of magic to become visible and doable. Here, in the backstage unfolds the drama of the origin of the *I* in a division, in a gap: a story of loss – the ground of theater as a *theoria* (view) of absence, of death. However, somewhere else, in a *different* space, in something that perhaps lacks the characteristics of space – is it a "black hole"? – is the kingdom of the Incomprehensible Void.

Now, much has been written about the "Impossible theater," grounded – or, rather, suspended – as it is in this non-space. From the perspective we have adopted here, theater's "Ground Zero" concerns what Freud, in a footnote again, calls the dream's undecipherable "navel":

> *There is at least one spot in every dream at which it is unplumbable – a navel, as it were, that is its point of contact with the unknown.*[27]

The dream's and the phantasy's point of contact with the unknown coincide. This is not theater's invisible core, but its un-visualizable core, not the locus of the origin of the *I*, but the locus of Origin, theater's metaphysical core. Others have spoken about it: Kant, as the unknowable "thing-in-itself," Bion, as the [O]rigin, Lacan, as the un-symbolizable Real. In this black hole of meaning, questions of "where," "why" and "what" are deprived of a referent (*privation*). Here we find ourselves in theater's ultimate battleground: the Un-representable.

Plato's mythic "theater" in his allegorical Myth of the Cave brings out in sharp relief our modern "nihilistic turn" following Nietzsche's pronouncement of the death of God, a turn further strengthened by our post-modern slippery relativism. This state of mind makes us more tolerant of the *aporiae* of the human intellect. The Platonic Myth underlines Plato's idealism. His prisoner can eventually contemplate the Sun (ultimate Reality, the eternal Forms), our modern spectator, however, has been made conscious of ultimate Reality's inaccessibility. This may be due, in part, to Freud's "Copernican revolution," coupled with a technological revolution that got out of hand and has dealt a cunningly concealed narcissistic blow to contemporary man. For Plato, however, the επεκεινα was accessible to humans – even though to the privileged few – and the reason for which he banished the tragedians from his ideal State was that he considered them to be obstacles in the path towards Truth. The tragedians exposed humanity's "blind spots" and that made them dangerous. The philosopher – that privileged, uncompromising "student of death"[28] – had no tolerance for ambiguities and ontological schisms, and, paradoxically, if not ironically, even less for blind spots, un-representables, black holes and Nothingness.

The un-representable core is the basis of theater's paradox as a *theoria* of what cannot be *theatron*. Blau[29] affirms: "There is something in the nature of theater which from the very beginning of theater has always resisted being theater." Maeterlinck's theater without actors or

Grotowski's theater without spectators represent responses to that struggle. *Αἴδης* ("Invisible") is, ultimately, un-visualizable. We shall, in Part II, look at one man's heroic (and doomed?) attempt to deal with theater's self-contradictory epistemic frustrations: Kantor's Theater of Death.

We have placed theater's edifice on the perpetually shifting ground of Winnicott's "intermediate area." In this in-between area of ambiguity, paradox and play, we find Aristotle's excluded middle, a middle that refuses to be excluded. This is also Plato's *χωρα*, Kristeva's *chora*, madness, as well as the territory of the foundation of the *I*. It is here in an amalgam of illusion and reality that the *I* makes its first appearance. Theater positions itself in the area of the emergence of the *I*. The *I* opens its eyes for the first time to discover a fluid world in constant oscillation between two realities that are mutually exclusive. "All the world's a stage" on either of the two sides of the eyelid/curtain, while the play that is being staged is always a tragedy.

For Winnicott, the intermediate area of being, located between oneness (motherinfant) and separation (me – not-me), is the area of all cultural phenomena. It is an area where boundaries are loose and indefinable, allowing a to-and-fro between union and separateness, a playful overlap between subject and object, between fantasy and reality, between presence and absence. This is the area of "creative living," permeated by what Winnicott calls the "female element." It is interesting to note that this concept of a "third space" lying in-between a primordial reality and the separate autonomous individual is a faithful echo of Plato's notion of a third area, *chora* (*χωρα*), which Plato describes as being open to everything, "*hardly real*" and "*apprehended only by spurious reason . . . as in a dream.*"[30] This is an all-receiving area which, as in Winnicott, has maternal characteristics and in which something can "be one and, also, two at the same time." Like Winnicott's intermediate area it admits of no destruction, it is "eternal."

It is in relation to this *chora* that Kristeva[31] describes the experience of the "abject." The sense of the abject arises in the encounter with the dead (m)Other. We regard the (m)Other as the part of the One that has become Other, i.e., alien, dead: Death. The encounter is characterized by a bewildering mixture of ecstatic *jouissance* and abject horror. The "spectator" of the abject, petrified, is torn between an uncanny attraction to abolish and an urgent need to re-instate the boundaries with the (m)Other. His is a struggle between a narcissistic centripetal return to fusion and one-ness with mother, and a centrifugal drive away towards the Other. Death awaits at both ends. The joy of re-fusion entails the horror of formlessness and existential collapse, the annihilation of the self, and so it must be resisted. From another perspective, the horror and aversion characteristic of the abject is related to the dread of collapse and fracture of the One and the inevitable dis-illusionment of separateness that follows as a necessary consequence. Kristeva's spectator of the abject is the Spectator, the space (*chora*) of the abject being the space of theater. Here, the spectator is infused with the materiality of death. The memory of the primal wound of rupture and loss is brought back by the (m)Other–ghost–actor. That memory has been "embodied" in an incorporeal ghost, giving substance to the shadow. Plato's notion of φαντασμα aptly refers to the ghost of "body memory" (σωματοειδες).[32] It is the shadow of the archaic, mutilated body, carrier of the ancient trauma, weighed down by the memory of its "earthy" corporeality, a visible aspect of the invisible and of the un-represented returning to demand its representation. It is the return of the dead who heeded the Orphic/Dionysian counsel and drank from the Spring of Remembrance. Memory links them back to the archaic body which, however, needs to be *spoken* if it is to be carried by the ghost and be represented (*mise-en-scène*). The dark Acheron must be crossed twice if this is to be achieved. Again, the wounded body must be exposed to violence for a second time, this time to the violence of language to become an *ombre parlante*.[33] Yet, the "speaking shadow" will only be able to speak a broken language recording the battle of the body with the word, displaying the scars of its genesis. The speech of the ghost is a narration of his/her autobiography of its schismatic origins, the archival memory of the primal laceration and loss, and a plea for the re-integration of a *corps morcelé*.

The ghost (actor) is a negative hallucination of the object as absent, the presence of the object's absence, a visualization of absence. The ghost is in search of its double (spectator) in order to re-integrate its fragmented body and come alive. This is the dynamic underlying the game of Freud's grandson, as well as Lacan's "mirror stage."[34]

Theater appears as a compulsion. Its intensity is maintained and endlessly fueled by the fact that behind the spectator's mirror image – momentarily captured – is the Un-representable. The actor-ghost is the spoken (and the speaking) shadow of the unspeakable. S/he is the *ersatz* representative of the Un-representable but cannot present it: the actor can only present an absence, the absence of the object, of something, whereas the Un-representable is a *No-thing*, inconceivable and un-symbolizable. So, far behind the absent object that is equated with death in the psyche, is Death that resists any *mise-en-scène*. Death as the prime signified without a signifier is a resident of Ground Zero, of the Incomprehensible Void, an *aporia* located in the third, deepest and most remote region of theater's architectural edifice. What Blanchot[35] said of art in general certainly applies to theater in particular as an act "mysteriously immobilized . . . between death as the possibility of understanding, and death as the horror of impossibility."

Heiner Müller[36] believed that the level of a culture is measured by its manner of dealing with the dead. The dead need to be liberated, he says, and it is the function of art to take care of the dead. Perhaps this is why theater is more important today when the dead are being "undone" by the media culture more than at any other time in our history. If the formula of theater, as Müller maintains,[37] is birth and death, it follows that, by enacting the birth–death event, theater, as theater of memory, is necrophilic: it is *a reparative dialogue with the dead*, a dialogue, ultimately, with the Un-representable.

Mystery rituals of Greek Antiquity, containing unmistakable inchoate elements of theater, revolved around an encounter with death, and effectuated a dialogue with the dead. This brought about a "reconciliation with death," according to Burkert.[38] Little Ernst's spool game, and especially his mirror image game staging his own appearance/disappearance, can be regarded as such a reparative attempt to integrate absence and reconcile with it. Identified with his absent self, Ernst is asserting: "*I am (not)*." Absence/Death is integrated into a "whole" jubilant but horrified self. In his double, the child sees his narcissistic Ideal and his annihilation, i.e., Death, simultaneously. In this casual game, Ernst staging his own duality becomes the first spectator of human ontological schism, the first theater spectator/actor. In Lacan's understanding, the boy's joy is anticipatory of an imagined unified, cohesive self that is yet to come and is directly linked to his sense of being presently broken up in pieces (*morcelé*). This discrepancy in the child's self image is a manifestation of a neotenic[39] fragmenting asynchrony in the course of human development. The mirror image is, thus, reassuring, but its disappearance in the play links it to the Un-representable with which it is contiguous. The mirror image is, after all, *reversed* and this makes it the absence of the absent, which leads to the core of the Un-representable. The jubilance at the moment of the re-appearance of the lost object/self may be no more than the result of a *Verneinung* of the underlying terror of annihilation. The child's fascination with such compulsive "peek-a-boo" games speaks to the traumatic nature of the experience reproduced.

Freud, as mentioned, considered the little boy's game with absence "a great cultural achievement." On the cultural anthropological scale, could we say that this elemental play that can be seen as the germ of the theatrical setting corresponds to the moment when, for the first time, Paleolithic man cast his gaze on a human corpse – or even on a dead animal body that he had hunted – and saw *his own image* reversed? Was he, consequently, seized by unspeakable terror? Could this coincide with the moment that man started burying his dead and engaged in funerary rituals, rituals that could be considered to be a form of proto-theater that carried a dialogue with the dead? The appearance of human burials in the Paleolithic period that marked such an intellectual and social leap for *homo sapiens* can be attributed to several reasons, but could an underlying psychic mechanism of *Verneinung* have, also, played a role, making burial the first instance of repression of a terrifying state? The dead are buried so they can be "forgotten." Patroklos complaint to Achilles was in effect: "You forgot to forget me!"

Funerary rituals associated with the burial of the dead – clearly repara-tive in their nature – uniformly reproduce or re-stage the violence of the loss as an attempt to come to terms with it. They, thus, have a theatrical aspect. We see this clearly in the *Iliad* (Book XXIII). Plutarch gives us a detailed description of the annual ceremonies in honor of those who fell "for the freedom of the Hellenes" in the battle of Plataeae against the invading Persians 600 years earlier![40] These activities involved the bloody ritual sacrifice of a black bull, its blood flowing over the pyre for the dead heroes to "take their fill" (cf. *Odyssey*, Book 11). The ritual activities re-enacted the atmosphere and violence of the battle, while the "spectators" of these activities were not only the living participants but the *stelae* of the dead as well, which were decorated, robed and treated as the guests of honor of the sacred ceremony. The dead were present, both as actors and as spectators.

More significantly, we must note the distinct elements of an *Ur-theater* that staged a dialogue with the dead in the practices of *Nekyiomanteia* of Classical Antiquity, such as the one at the banks of the river Acheron and the Acherousian Lake in Thesprotia.[41] Excavations, there, showed a complex building arrangement of labyrinthine dark rooms and an under-ground arched Hall, probably the site of the pre-historic cult cave. Here was believed to be the entrance to the Underworld, to the Kingdom of the Dead. The visitors that came to consult the shadows of the dead who were able to foresee the future had to undergo a rigorous physical and spiritual preparation that would enable them to communicate with the ghosts. The pilgrims would eventually be led to the Hall of Images and, here, the ghosts of the departed would make their appearance and speak to them. The significant and striking archeological find in this Hall was a collection of small wheels, ratchets and catapults, while in the adjacent room several iron weights, weighing about 10 kilograms each, were dis-covered. The thick walls of the sanctuary contained concealed spaces and passages. It seems, therefore, that the priests hidden in the spaces behind the walls would manipulate machinery that used wheels, pulleys and counterweights to lower images of the dead from the ceiling at the end of the Hall to the dreadful awesome amazement of the stunned spectators. Magic, the sacred and theater meet here. It is, also, interesting that *ex votos* depicting Dionysos–Hades and Persephone were found at the site. Dionysos, Persephone's son, re-appears here, again, as the god of death.

Dionysos will appear again as the ceremonial Master (*Iakchos*) of blood, death and birth in the prime religious manifestation of Athenian life, the Eleusinian Mysteries which, also, involved unmistakable theatrical practices in the context of death and loss. Here, too, the dead Kore will return from the dead and appear in front of ek-static worshippers, possibly through an "intervention" of the hierophants similar to that of their Thesprotian colleagues. We have several bits of information from diverse sources about the various events that took place in the course of the Great Mysteries, but the Mysteries still guard their secrecy as we have no indication of how these events related to each other and in what sequence they occurred. The essential theme, however, and the core event of the nighttime festivities, was the death and descent to the Underworld of Demeter's daughter, Kore/Persephone – following a violent rupture of the mother–child bond that points to the primal phantasy as described here – and Kore's return from the dead to the joy of the celebrant *mystae*. Our sources allude to infanticide, gruesome sacrifices, mysterious sexual ritual activities, a sacred marriage between the hierophant and the priestess, sacred "calls," a miraculous birth, etc. All these events revolved around a core sacred act, the αρρητον, the "unspeakable" (un-representable?), that tied everything together, which, however, remains unknown. However, of particular relevance is the nature and manner of Kore's return from Hades, which took place in the dark Telesterion dimly lit by a central fire. Was it a vision, a ghost-like apparition to the initiates, a hallucination as the result of the *kykeon* they had drunk or was it a "shape" (σχημα) or a statuette of the Kore brought in by the priests among the wavering shadows of the Hall? If a concrete object were used, we would have, here, another instance of a mystical proto-theater as that performed in the *Nekyiomanteia*.

A reparative encounter with the dead (the re-appearance of the "lost object"), however, can also occur via "shades" of the mind: in dreams. Here, the ghosts of the mind and theater's ghost actors overlap and coincide, but on the dream stage no material objects are needed. The dreamer creates his own actors and is himself an actor, spectator and *metteur-en-scène* all at once. Such is the scene in Book XXIII of the *Iliad*. Achilles falling asleep on the shore – on that indeterminate vague shifting boundary between land and sea, between reality and phantasy – sees the image of the dead Patroklos and the two engage in a dialogue with each other within that "in-between space" of primordial fluidity. If we see elements of a proto-theater in this spectation, it is important to take note of the fact that the experience is intrinsically linked to *mourning*. Achilles' dialogue with the dead is driven by his need to come to terms with loss. He attempts this by re-staging the trauma: the re-appearance of the lost narcissistic object[42] achieves the momentary re-establishment of the broken relationship but is immediately followed by the incomprehensible traumatic shatter of their union. Patroklos is there, but he is now Other. "Stupefied" (ταφων), Achilles springs up, smiting his hands together to grasp No-thing. This moment of shock in front of the incomprehensible Void is expressed in the Greek text by the word ταφος, a word that, semantically, refers both to "burial," as well as to a sense of "daze" or overwhelming amazement.[43] Here, it is Achilles who is the prototypical spectator and actor of the enactment of the originary rupture of the unity of his being. Moreover, it is in the context of mourning that theater restages the ontological split that constitutes the *first play*. This will be repeated compulsively thereafter. Pentheus – the "pathological" mourner – delved into his unconscious (κρυφαιοι χοροι) in order to be the spectator of the fragmentation that he had refused to re-member. Does every spectator-Pentheus – we ask – leave the theater at the end fragmented?

The image of the dead Patroklos, like the images of the dead in the *Nekyiomanteion*, the ghost the double, the Other, the Actor, all *indicate* our foundational ontological schism and are *images of Death*.

Notes

1 P. Lacoue-Labarthe, "Theatricum Analyticum," *Glyph*, 2, 1977: 136.
2 "The ego is first and foremost a body ego" (Freud, *S.E.* 19: 26)
3 cf. the myth of the violent bisection of the *androgynon* in Plato (Plato, 1973, *Symposium*, 189e).
4 It is interesting to note the evidence that, as far back as the beginning of the second millennium BCE and possibly even earlier, the dismemberment theme was enacted in Egyptian rituals (δεικελα) lamenting the mutilation of Osiris. See E. Rozik, *The Roots of Theatre* (Iowa City: U. of Iowa P., 2002), 315ff.
5 H. Blau, *Blooded Thought* (New York: Performing Arts Journal Publications, 1982), 150.
6 R. Schechner, *The Future of Ritual* (New York: Routledge, 2003)
7 Isaacs (1948).
8 Of note here are some intriguing recent findings from the field of neuroscience: a category of neurons was discovered in the brain, the so-called "mirror neurons," which are activated both when the subject is observing a certain act performed by another and when the subject himself/herself is performing the same act. Further, the same neurons are activated when the subject is *imagining* performing that act. These findings seem to provide the neurological basis of an archaic state of undifferentiation between self and Other

(the state of the fusional One), as well as of the consequent *subjectivity* of alterity (following the fracture of the One). In addition, they demonstrate the capacity of the mind (imagination/phantasy) to *reflect* the body in its undifferentiated mirror state. See P. F. Ferrari and G. Rizzolatti, "Mirror neuron research: the past and the future," *Philos. Trans. Royal Soc. London B Biol. Sci.* 369, 1644, 2014: 20130169.

9 Lorenz (1967).
10 How the infant feels is obviously impossible to know. Attempted descriptions of very early states of infancy are assumptions (fantasies?) based on retroactive insights from the analysis of children and adults.
11 Bion (1984).
12 Freud, *S.E.* 18: 14–16.
13 The "primal curtain"?
14 Lacan (1966), 97.
15 M. Heidegger, *The Question of Being*, trans. W. Kluback and J. Wilde (New York: Twayne, 1958).
16 A. Artaud, *Le théâtre et son double* (Paris: Gallimard, 1938).
17 We assume the existence of the Unconscious following the appearance of organized communities of *homo sapiens*, if not earlier.
18 K.I. Arvanitakis, "Dipl' ereo (A tale of doubles) *The Bacchae*," in *The Theban Cycle*, ed. C. Yiallouridis (Athens: European Cultural Centre of Delphi, 2007), 247–254.
19 J. Grotowski, *Towards a Poor Theater* (New York: Simon and Schuster, 1968).
20 Schechner (2003); also, *Performance Theory* (New York: Routledge, 1988).
21 H-T. Lehmann, *Postdramatic Theater*, trans. K. Jürs-Munby (New York: Routledge, 2006).
22 E. Fischer-Lichte, *Theater, Sacrifice, Ritual* (New York: Routledge, 2005).
23 E. Wright, "Psychoanalysis and the theatrical: analyzing performance," in *Analysing Performance*, ed. P. Campbell (Manchester: Manchester U. P., 1996), 175–190.
24 F. Decreus, *The Ritual Theater of Theodoros Terzopoulos* (New York: Routledge, 2018).
25 Rozik (2002).
26 Bion (1984), 36.
27 Freud, *S.E.* 4: 111.
28 Plato (1973), *Phaedo*, 81a1.
29 H. Blau, *The Eye of Prey* (Indiana U. P., 1987), 165.
30 Plato (1973), *Timaeus*, 52.
31 J. Kristeva, *Pouvoirs de l' horreur* (Paris: Seuil, 1980). J. Kristeva, *Polylogue* (Paris: Seuil, 1977).
32 Plato (1973), *Phaedo*, 81c8–81d4.
33 P. Aulagnier, *La violence de l'interprétation* (Paris: P.U.F., 1975).
34 Lacan (1966), 93–100.
35 M. Blanchot, *L' espace littéraire* (Paris: Gallimard, 1955).
36 H. Müller, *Gasammelte Irrtümer* (Berlin: Verlag der Autoren, 1996), 3: 214–230.
37 H. Müller, *Germania* (New York: Semiotext(e), 1990), 56.
38 Burkert (1983), 295.
39 Neoteny refers to the condition of the human infant's anatomic prematurity at birth.

40 *Ibid.*, 56.
41 K.I. Arvanitakis, "Nekromanteio Theatro," in *Kathodos*, ed. T. Terzopoulos (Kiato: Katagramma, 2011), 280–287.
42 Patroklos' request that Achilles have their funerary ashes placed together in the same coffer – in the golden amphora that Achilles' mother had given him – so that they could be one as they had been in life, suggests that the relationship between Achilles and Patroklos had a fusional character.
43 Even though the gender differs in the two cases: masculine (*o*) for "burial," neuter (*το*) for "stupefaction."

4 Why theater

This question concerning a universal human practice could be taken as a search for an explanation of something we instinctively need to *do*. Yet, theater is not something we do but rather what we *are*. We are the schism, the duality we re-present, again and again, in an endless chain of theater-within-theater. Freud, within a frame of a mechanistic energy model, believed that by repetition we aim at a degree of mastery of a trauma through "binding" or eliminating the excessive excitation caused by it. The trauma in question here is the primal scene of origins as the result of a division. The *I* is born as *I* and as *Other*, as present and as absent, as living and as dead. This primal scene is staged again and again in an agonizing attempt to re-work it, to "bind" the traumatic excitation that results from it.

The actor, an ordinary human being, enters the stage and instantly becomes, say, the Officer in Stringberg's *Dreamplay*: Bergman confesses to being stunned by the magic of that moment.[1] This mysterious transformation is unfathomable, it is wonder, and it is the root of the sacred. The transformation is ultimately, of course, to death, to the flip side of being. The *Other* is the locus of Death. In the primary phantasy, at the moment of the original rupture, the part of the no-longer unitary self that had now become estranged and Other was a *dead self*. What follows is a series of interminable attempts to re-unite or at least integrate the now irreversibly divided and consequently conflicting parts of the self to reconcile them and to achieve a degree of continuity (Alkmaeon's "joining the beginning to the end") – attempts that are repeatedly frustrated. This sad but vital chain of doomed attempts we call life's theater, and it is what makes theater life.

Theater as a search for the lost part of the self, for what can only return as a dead object, a shadow, a simulacrum, a ghost, turns our question of *Why theater* to "*Why nekyia*." An irresistible drive to dialogue with the dead characterizes *homo sapiens* since the dawn of civilization. Why?

Once ontological division takes place, conflict arises as an inevitable consequence. In the West, as we saw, an early attempt to deal with the conflict that an individual necessarily faces as a divided existence took the form of tragedy. Tragedy is, fundamentally, a dialogue with the invisible, with death – death that always occurs *behind* the visible stage. Hegel,[2] in his theory of tragedy, held an optimistic view of conflict resolution that was embedded in the idealism of his times and upheld the fundamental unity of Being and Nothing. This led him to believe that both inter-personal (e.g., in *Antigone*) as well as intra-personal (e.g., in *Oedipus Rex*) tragic oppositions between two positions that are equally valid could be reconciled (*versöhnt*) in a synthesis that restores the unity of the self and establishes moral order. Tragedy, he thought, brings about "a reconcili-ation in the soul of the spectator," and, thus, "life can heal its wounds again."[3] Moral reconciliation is, of course, a reflection of meta-physical reconciliation. While Hegel's concern was the ethical reconciliation of the two sides within a divided self, Aristotle's interest was in the "puri-fication" (*κάθαρσις*) of emotions that he believed tragedy brings about. This was a more explicitly psychological focus on the foundations of morality. Tragic conflict generates emotions like pity, fear, hatred, envy, longing, etc. and these must be brought to a "mean," to an intermediate area where the opposite extremes meet, thereby attaining the essence of virtue. This is an emotional reconciliation.[4] *Ethos*, Aristotle believed, can be achieved through repetition and practice.[5] The moral question, however, in both Hegel and Aristotle, acquires its meaning only within the meta-physical order of death.

The philosopher's reconciliation of opposing moral, meta-physical or psychological forces in tragedy pivoted on death – forces that, in fact, describe what we might call, today, "positions" in the Kleinian sense of relational modes – corresponds to the psychoanalyst's concept of *psychic integration* of discrepant and conflicting parts of the self. Is this what is sought in all theater, and does this explain theater's universality?

Winnicott[6] hypothesized that our initial, pre-psychic state so to speak, was an unthinkable frightful state of *un-integration*. The fear of falling back into that state of "primitive agonies" accompanies us throughout life, yet it is experienced as something that might happen in the future, occluding the fact that it has already happened in our forgotten archaic past. The moment of rupture experienced when the primary object (or its later substitutes) is absent threatens to reactivate that original state of un-integration. This is the terror of falling into Bion's "O," i.e., into something formless, ineffable and unspeakably dreadful. The O[rigin] is inherently unknowable and corresponds to what we have called, here, the Un-representable – only its "evolution" into fantasies, myths, religions or scientific theories can be known. Can we say that the theatrical setting aims to promote the integration of the fragments that resulted from the primal ontological schism and, consequently, diminish the fears of falling into the chaotic agonies of un-integration? Is this, in the end, theater's attempt to heal the original trauma?

The question is how theater could achieve this. Dread results from the expectation of a precipitous return to the archaic un-organized pre-mental body. Insofar as the body embodies absence it is constitutionally vulnerable at any moment to fall into that state. Theater stages and thereby promotes such a return to what is, in fact, the Artaldian body of primitive violence, the "body in flames." The theatrical setting, consisting of a solid frame composed of a set of socio-psychological codes, acts as a "container" in Bion's sense,[7] a circumscribed space that "contains" and processes the crude terrifying persecutory elements of the un-organized original body. This allows and promotes the formation of thought and of symbols that make absence (Death) more tolerable. The creation of *meaning* is now possible, and this would counteract the meaningless "nameless dread." For Badiou,[8] "theater is the greatest machine ever invented for absorbing contradictions." Turri,[9] insightfully, elucidates theater's containment further by proposing that it is through the operation of alpha-function[10] in the actor-spectator dyad that an integrated and enriched sense of the self can arise.

The basic thesis here is that theater attempts a "regressive" return to the original trauma in order to repeat the sequence of events that followed it and thereby re-work (*Durcharbeiten*) the various healing processes of that wound, making its indelible scars more tolerable.

Aulagnier's schema[11] may be helpful in conceptualizing how this can take place. Her theory elucidates some important features of the developmental process leading to the organization of an original state of chaos and to the creation of meaning. She stresses the problematic relation of the body to language which is, in fact, a relationship of violence. Theater can be seen as a titanic battle between the body and the word. Aulagnier postulates a developmental sequence of three dynamic states that she calls *causalités*. During the first one, the *originaire*, the body – an "extraterritoriality" to the psyche – produces "pictograms" (cf. Artaud's "hieroglyphs") which are, in fact, pre-representational, unthinkable (i.e., cannot be made the object of thought) and unknowable bodily schemata that will, later, provide the ground of representation. This stage is before the differentiation between *I* and *not-I*, and hence the source of all aggression is felt to be within the self. At moments of physiological disequilibrium, the body self is attacked as a persecutor and pictograms of violent mutilation, self-annihilation and disintegration arise. These will re-emerge in later life at moments of stress, of creation, of madness, or on stage. In the *originaire*, we are – as with Winnicott's un-integration and Bion's "O" – in the territory of the Un-representable. In this context mother's linguistic intervention – indeed intrusion – occurs. Through her "act of speech," the *infans* ("lacking speech") becomes a "spoken shadow" (*ombre parlé*). Mother will "speak the body" of her infant, viz., bathe her baby in language, "voice" her child in all spheres of emotion, stimulating and verbalizing every bodily zone, thereby imposing a categorically heterogeneous order on the infant's bodily being that constitutes violence. This is the moment of a radical ontological conflict produced by a violence that Aulagnier calls "primal," viz., the collision between two unrelated and irreconcilable categories, physical and linguistic. In the stages that follow, those of *primaire* and of *secondaire*, when differentiation of *I* and *not-I* appears, the child will be able to produce scenic representations of bodily events (*mise-en-scène*) to record his/her history, and, later, ideic representations to give it meaning (*mise-en-sens*). The developed *I* of the *secondaire* – now a "speaking shadow" (*ombre parlante*) – is the space of self-historization and of identity. However, all this is unattainable without the structuring primal violence. The speaking subject will always carry the body memory of the violent impact of an alien extraterritorial force that transposed it onto another register. Owing to this, mother tongue is, fundamentally, a foreign language; the task of mutual translation is never-ending, while what is lost never vanishes. The Other, on this plane, is language, language that signifies the death of the body. Viewed from the perspective of Aulagnier's theory, we would maintain that theater emerges as the *I* is compelled to consolidate itself by re-staging its traumatic autobiography, its archaic pre-symbolic body states, thereby investing them with meaning.

The problem of life, for Winnicott, is the problem of dealing with loss. Something is left behind in order to move forward but is never given up, so the *I* in its path is always pulled simultaneously in two opposite directions in a perpetual tug of war. The task of life, then, is to create a space where the two antithetical forces can co-exist, a space where each can see itself as the mirror image of the other. This is the theatrical space, an "in-between" space where a play of "lost and found" can unfold, where lost (dead) objects/parts of the self can be recaptured, if only in effigy. Psychoanalysis has assiduously labored to construct a model – a myth that we call "theory" – to describe this dynamic state of affairs. The psychoanalytic model attempts to talk about something that in fact resists language. Language comes as an *après coup* to impose form on what is essentially pre-verbal. In theory-building, psychoanalysis repeats not only the primary violence of psychological development, but also the function of theater that mirrors it. As for the practice of psychoanalysis, isn't the psychoanalytic setting[12] a space of theater?

The Kleinian model[13] is centered on the transition, or rather, the perpetual oscillation between an initial relational state characterized by splitting, fragmentation and the dominance of the death instinct and a subsequent state of coalescence of part-objects to form a whole object – and concurrently a whole subject – that entails guilt, depressive anxieties and attempts at reparation. The very status of the "object" is the materialization and concretization of a traumatic gap resulting from an ontological schism *ab initio*. The ego, defined by the gap, seeks the object, of necessity, from the very beginning. The absent object absorbs into itself the forces of the death instinct and is felt as sadistically persecuting the self. It is the gradual integration into the self of the absent ("bad") object and the toleration of loss, lack and otherness that will permit the formation of a whole object/ subject. The object will be accepted as being both present *and* absent, both loving *and* hating, both within me *and* without me, both me *and* Other – matters relevant to the theatrical setting. Notably, the whole subject, no longer split, incorporates two valences, and is subject to ambivalence, balancing between two poles. In the end, as the schism between subject and object is better tolerated, Death is seen as the condition of life.[14]

It could, thus, be said that, in Kleinian terms, the theatrical setting reflects an effort to construct a whole object insofar as it brings together in a mutually mirroring relationship the present and the absent object; and, concurrently, to construct a whole subject insofar as it apposes the *I* and the *not-I* in a mirroring relationship. Theater clearly belongs to the space of the depressive position.

We advance, therefore, that the aim of theater is not primarily the moderated cathartic release of repressed impulses by lowering resistances which is the classical view,[15] but the integration of the fragments of the self into a whole *I*. Post-Freudian theater is pre-symbolic and pre-oedipal, centered on the not-yet-integrated subject in a maternal sundered universe. "Theatricality [is] a necessary element in the construction of the subject," as Wright avers.[16]

In the coming together of the various fragments of the self, an important role is played by reparation, ultimately the reparation of the existential tear. Hanna Segal[17] considers that all art aims at re-creating a lost world and is, therefore, rooted in the depressive position. The phantasy of having destroyed the object by one's vicious attacks leads to despair, guilt and the need to repair and restore the lost object. Segal makes reference to Proust according to whom the artist creates because of his longing to recover a lost world. The lost world, from the perspective that we have adopted here, is the original One of the primal phantasy before its division that resulted in ontological duality. It is the lost, dead parts of the self that are left behind. In Segal's view, the artist accepts the reality of death of the object and of the self, and gives full expression to the conflict and the union between the death instinct and the life instinct. It may be more accurate to say that the artist *struggles* to achieve this, that art is precisely that struggle, a determined fight to reach a goal that remains elusive. And although this may be true of all art, it is particularly true of theater – and this in a direct way – the reason being that theater, as has been mentioned, focuses directly on the body, on the archaic body which is the territory and subject of fragmentation and loss. The body is the field of the operation of the death instinct and of the life instinct that emerges out of it.

The toleration of loss, of the absence of the object, of the object as dead, is facilitated by the creation of symbols which appear within the frame of the depressive position. Symbols[18] as monuments of absence are essentially reparative to the dead object. They are not attempts at restitution of what is lost; they acknowledge their status as a shadow, the memory of a scar that can never be made to disappear. In indicating both the presence and the absence of the object symbols can be said to be whole objects. They constitute the transparent substance of the actor.

What is the relevance of all this to the question "Why theater"? Theater stages, in compulsive repetitions, the original trauma of the ontological schism and struggles to re-work it and attain an integrated, meaningful wholeness.[19]

However, what does "re-work" really mean? Does theater struggle to revive the dead objects/parts of the self, to repair them, to enter into a dialogue with them, to mourn them, to punish them, to let them die, to join them in death, to bury them, to forgive them? Are all these forms of "integration" of the existential gap? To turn around the mask and enter the ου-τοπια of the Other('s) space? The τοπος of radical alterity of the "whole subject"? Else, why re-stage the wound? Is this ontological masochism or eroticization of Death? In search of a forever elusive identity?

It would seem that deadened parts of the self, ghosts of murdered objects return in theater, as they do in dreams, in rituals, in madness. They emerge desperately seeking to be re-animated, seeking revenge, seeking to be forgotten, to be allowed to die, seeking re-union with the living or with the dead. Torn between being and not-being, between the past (One-ness) and the present (schism), they abolish time so they can re-establish the original Unity that is immobilized in Death's eternity (*Todestrieb*). Yet, they hope to be infused with life, to become "blooded thoughts," to be integrated with the living and be allowed to carry their shadowy scarred existence among the living, to live through linear time, to become *mnesic*, rather than *ana-mnesic*, until they are eventually granted nothingness.

We conclude that the effort towards constructing an integrated whole subject, a subject conscious of its identity in division and fragmentariness, of its mobile center of gravity, of its paradoxical nature situated at a continually shifting frontier between Being and Nothing (Hegel), between raw physical reality and symbol, between hatred and compassion, between chaos and meaning, yet a subject that is a malleable and resilient unit tolerant of loss and capable of "creative living,"[20] must be recognized as theater's principal project, a project whose outcome remains forever uncertain. Mourning and toleration of loss is at the center of it.

The project has, unquestionably, a "therapeutic" character and this is recognized by thinkers and theater people from Aristotle to Grotowski. Grotowski, for example, stresses the integrative function of theater which he considers as a form of therapy in acquiring self-awareness.[21] The aim is self-discovery. As for Aristotle, the discovery of identity is the principal gain from *mimesis*, and he believes this explains the pleasure derived from imitation that forms the basis of art:

> *For it is for this reason that men take pleasure in seeing a likeness, that in contemplating it* [θεωρουντας] *they happen to learn and conclude what each thing is, for instance, that this man is that man.*[22]

The same holds for the spectator *himself* contemplating his own likeness (the actor) and discovering his own identity.

If the search for an integrated identity is theater's underlying project, the risks involved in the process are substantial. There can be no spectation with impunity. Pentheus reminds us of that. This is because human identity is founded on an archaic wound that borders on the Un-representable. Theater returns to the fragmented, dis-membered body, "signaling in flames" and balancing precariously at the edge of an abyss that threatens to pull it into the incomprehensible Void – the *arreton* that resists the stage. If the question is asked "Why do we make theater," the answer would, surely, have to be "in order not to fall into madness."

Notes

1 I. Bergman, *Lanterna Magica* (Paris: Gallimard, 1987).
2 Hegel (1967), 736–743.
3 G.F. Hegel, *Aesthetics. Lectures on Fine Arts*, trans. T. M. Knox (Oxford: Clarendon Press, 1975).
4 Which allows pity to act as a civilizing force, according to C. F. Alford, *The Psychoanalytic Theory of Tragedy* (New Haven and London: Yale U. P., 1992).

5 Aristotle, *Nicomachean Ethics*, trans. H. Rackham (Cambridge, MA: Harvard U. Press, 1982), 70–95.

6 D.W. Winnicott, *Through Paediatrics to Psychoanalysis* (London: Hogarth, 1975).

7 Bion (1984).

8 A. Badiou, *Éloge du théâtre* (Paris: Flammarion, 2013), 25.

9 M.G. Turri, *Acting, Spectating and the Unconscious: A Psychoanalytic Perspective on Unconscious Processes of Identification in the Theater* (New York: Routledge, 2017).

10 Bion (1984).

11 Aulagnier (1975).

12 i.e., the physical-psychological format of sessions at regular intervals in which the analysand lies on the couch free associating and the analyst, invisible, is sitting behind. The body is immobilized so that the archaic body can battle with speech, time and absence.

13 M. Klein, *Envy and Gratitude & Other Works* (New York: Delta, 1977). Also, M. Klein, *Love, Guilt and Reparation & Other Works* (New York: Delta, 1977).

14 We note that in the Kleinian model innate destructive psychic forces (Thanatos) that are responsible for division and fragmentation set the stage at the very beginning, with the forces of union (Eros) coming into play later. As Freud held, the Death instinct is older than Eros.

15 Green (1969).

16 Wright (1996), 189.

17 H. Segal, *Dream, Phantasy and Art* (New York: Routledge, 1991).

18 Συμβολον (συν-βολον) in ancient Greece referred to a fragment of an inscribed tablet that had been broken in two, each fragment being kept by each of two friends that had been separated, and representing the absent friend.

19 K.I. Arvanitakis, "A theory of theater: theater as theory," *Psychoanal. Contemp. Thought*, 1998: 33–60.

20 Winnicott (1971), 65–85.

21 Grotowski (1968), 255–257.

22 Butcher (1951), 1448b15–17, 14. Translation by the author.

Part II

5 Kantor's Theater of Death

We have argued that theater has its roots in a universal unconscious phantasy of a traumatic "primal scene" of the origin of the self as the result of a rupture of a primordial One. The self was, thus, born as a divided entity. The primordial schism engraved on the *I* a sense of ontological loss. The *I*, constituted of two inseparable parts – ultimately, a *living I* and a *dead I* – is positioned at the border between two distinct and opposing realities and charged with the lifelong task of devising means of relating one to the other as a condition for its survival – a continuous effort in a constantly shifting landscape. We advanced that the theatrical setting emerged as an attempt to deal with the archaic trauma of origins and consequent ontological division, to invest it with meaning and to construct a livable sense of identity that is tolerant of its inherent contradictions.

Tadeusz Kantor was a significant figure in twentieth-century theater who proposed a radically new way of experiencing the theatrical setting. Kantor's preoccupation with the foundational elements of theater, with different levels of reality, with death, irreversible loss and afterlife, with time and the indelible traces of memory, is by no means surprising. He was the product of a culture that built its identity on trauma, rupture, division and loss, and this on multiple levels: ethnic, social, historical, religious. Poland, as the result of repeated partitions survived only as a "thought," for almost a century-and-a-half a *sema*[1] signifying a glorious past that remained alive,[2] but – deep in the collective unconscious – only as a skeleton of history, like Kazimierz Wielki in Wyspiański's stained glass window of the then recently exhumed skeleton of the king.[3] Birth, death and resurrection shaped the national character of this "Christ of Nations" and found their pure expression in the deep religious feeling of every Pole.

Wielopole, the small Galician town in which Kantor was born and spent his early childhood years, was a community in which two cultures,

Catholics and Jews, lived, celebrated and suffered together the blows of history for centuries. Brought up in the presbytery of his mother's uncle, the parish priest, Kantor witnessed colorful Christian masses and festivities, and equally mysterious Jewish rituals and ceremonies, all taking place around the small town square, and leaving a lasting impression on the sensitive little boy. "I grew up in the shadow of the Catholic church and the synagogue," he will, later, reminisce. He saw himself as a Catholic, but also as "an old Spanish Jew," as he called himself in a letter to Achille Perilli.[4] His was a world of shifting identities and dialogues across cultures, Russian, Austrian, Polish, Roman Catholic, Ukrainian Greek Orthodox, Jewish, across fluid and porous boundaries in a little town that was granted the prerogative of insignificance, that of "facing eternity."[5]

Borders and boundaries (geographic, spiritual), and the causes of such divisions, i.e., wars and destruction, marked Kantor's psyche. Born in the midst of the First World War ("millions of corpses in the absurd hecatomb"), he is a mature man when, a quarter of a century later, another World War breaks out ("genocide, concentration camps, crematories, human beasts, death"[6]). A landscape of collapsed worlds and the specter of death dominated his vision:

> In times of madness created by men, in times of war, death and its frightening troupes . . . burst into and merged with the sphere of life.[7]

It was the pressing task of Kantor's generation to create a meaning of that mysterious and incomprehensible entanglement of life with death, a meaning that would permit the continuation of life, or of the fragments that were left behind. In the language of our times, Romanska[8] argues that Kantor's theater, like Grotowski's, represent "the purest theatrical expression of PTSD" (post-traumatic stress disorder), a theater that sought to "process the trauma of the Holocaust." I would agree, but suggest – in view of what has been said above – that the War events and the resulting socio-cultural disruption and fragmentation were events that re-activated an archaic primal trauma and provided the energy for the powerful creative outburst, the pathos, agony, bewilderment and absurdity that characterize both Grotowski's and Kantor's theater. The Holocaust was the traumatic "realization" of the most archaic "un-symbolizable" phantasy which, irrupting into the real, transformed it into the Lacanian Real.

Kantor's father was drafted at the outbreak of the First World War and never returned to his family after the end of hostilities. We find little Tadeusz frequently playing in cemeteries:

I would believe what I was told,
that is, that people live there underground.
                    (*Silent Night*)[9]

Marian Kantor returns again and again in Kantor's plays and, first and foremost, as Odysseus. The Second Coming or Last Judgment is a recurring theme in his plays: the dead will return – a belief reinforced by the teachings of the Church and by popular folklore. The Holy Mass every Sunday, at Christmas and Easter, is all about birth, death, the *other* life invisible, and the return of the dead. Little Tadeusz took all this in, full of fascination and wonderment. The Holy Mass was, in fact, his first exposure to theater. He remembers, at age four or five, re-enacting the Mass at the Presbytery Hall, he in a white shirt playing the Priest, with his sister helping him. The spectators were Uncle Joseph the town's priest, grandmother and mother.[10] In Kantor's theater, the "altar," as the "threshold between HEAVEN AND EARTH," is the altar of memory where a "mystical process," a Mass, unfolds (*Memory*).[11]

This sacred "Theater of Death" of the Church was a condensation and, at the same time, an expansion of the actual socio-historical theater of suffering and redemption that determined Kantor's view of the world and his conception of the task of art. A painter who, in effect, theatricalizes his canvases by "painting," as it were, moving yet lifeless bodies on stage, Kantor focuses *directly* on the disruptions, ruptures and vicissitudes of existence and of reality. The "REAL" is memory, ultimately memory of a deadly event inscribed on the body, and art springs out of death's reality and seeks to re-present it, i.e., by repeating it ("repetition is the essence of art," Kantor says in *Illusion and Repetition*[12]). Life, he insisted, cannot be expressed in art other than through the absence of life and a recourse to death.

It, thus, seems that, because of a host of hazardous circumstances, Kantor was destined to give us a theater focused on the very nature of theater, on its essence, a meta-theater recalling Euripides' *Bacchae*, a theater of the ontological imperative of division, mutilation and *penthos*.

Theater, in Kantor, is always a repetition: it follows and "repeats" an original traumatic event that has been lost in the dark recesses of memory, an event, however, that is "intuitively felt by the poets."

Since the beginning of my artistic life
this image
has always lived in me
deep inside me
. . .
Now I want to pull it out

. . .
Today, I realize that this un-conscious image
has always been rupturing
through those conscious activities.
                    (Silent Night)[13]

Art strives to integrate those unconscious images, as its highest goal is the freedom to

embrace the TOTAL HUMAN CONDITION
. . .
that is, PSYCHIC REGIONS OF A HUMAN BEING,
their depth, their immeasurable strength . . .
                    (Milano Lessons, No. 12)[14]

This, he says, is the most significant discovery of the twentieth century – a discovery referable to Freud's discovery of the centrality of *psychic* reality and the Unconscious.

Kantor, accordingly, believes that we have

two images, one that comes from our reality and the other from the world "beyond," which are imposed on each other. This process of achieving a total picture was almost a mysterious ritual.
                    (Theatrical Place)[15]

He was convinced that genuine creativity stems from a state of nostalgia for a "paradise lost," for a transcendental union with a lost world, and a sense of failure to achieve it "that can be found at the roots of ancient tragedy" (*Theatrical Place*).[16] This led him to a theater that turns its gaze towards the *heterotopia* of "that other world, . . . the regions pushed aside by sanctioned consciousness."[17] He defined the essence of theater as follows:

Theater is the place that reveals – like some ford in the river – the traces of a passage from that other side to our life.
    In the eyes of the spectator, the actor presents himself as having assumed the condition of a DEAD person. The spectacle, by its very nature, akin to a ritual or a ceremony, produces a shock that I would gladly characterize as metaphysical.[18]

This *other* world is an alien world of dead objects ("objects" in the psychoanalytic sense), dead parts of the self, a world in which Kantor locates the "REAL." Thus, he redefines the essential meaning of the relationship between spectator and actor:

IT IS NECESSARY TO RECOVER THE PRIMEVAL FORCE OF THE SHOCK TAKING PLACE AT THE MOMENT WHEN OPPOSITE A HUMAN (A SPECTATOR) THERE STOOD FOR THE FIRST TIME A HUMAN (AN ACTOR), DECEPTIVELY SIMILAR TO US, YET AT THE SAME TIME INFINITELY FOREIGN, BEYOND AN IMPASSABLE BARRIER.

(*The Theater of Death*)[19]

This scene evokes a primeval scene, retained somewhere in phylogenetic memory, of early *homo sapiens* who looked at a dead human and, for the first time, recognized himself, came face-to-face with his *other self.* Kantor's actor embodies the condition of the dead, the irreversible and fundamental difference between the living and the dead *I* and actualizes the moment of recognition that it is *I* who is alien or dead. The actor is my double: *I-dead.* "Confronted with our own image," Kantor adds, "we must become REUNITED."[20] This encounter with the dead *I* brings about a "meta-physical seizure" and provides the foundation of the sacred. The *I*, assuming its tragic dividedness, is caught between fascination and repulsion (Kristeva's *abject*).

True theater, "deeply rooted in the 'world beyond'," is

an activity that occurs if life is pushed to its final limits where all categories and concepts lose their meaning; . . . where madness, fever, hysteria and hallucinations are the last barricades of life before the approaching TROUPES OF DEATH and death's GRAND THEATER.

(*Theatrical Place*)[21]

Theater, in this view, is our last defense against the forces of death (the death drive) that inhabit the "other world" (the Unconscious).

It is clear from the above that Kantor's project has much in common with the psychoanalyst's. Their common aim is to break through the barrier of illusions of everyday life and reach the "inaccessible regions of the mind," where a different truth appears, a truth that is "cruel, brutal, wild."[22] This different truth is qualified as "real," as the ultimate truth behind appearances. Both, Kantor and the psychoanalyst, agree that there is a therapeutic gain from this ("so that we can cope better with our lives," says Kantor in *Reflection*[23]). Like the late Freud, and along the lines of the Kleinian school, the emphasis in Kantor is on Thanatos, rather than Eros. Significantly, both Freud and Kantor saw themselves as *conquistadores*, as daring explorers of new regions, and as revolutionaries challenging the falsely reassuring layers of superficial reality that is illusory and conceals a deeper truth.

The "psychology of the inner reaches" seeking the "deep layers of reality" arrives at a point where time is warped, shrunk.[24] This is the point zero of the psycho-soma where beginning and end coincide, where birth and death are one, where the primal scene is also the final scene. Here is the locus of the originary trauma which is the root of theatrical activity. Kantor directly addresses this "mythic" unconscious event in *Silent Night*,[25] a cricotage staged at Avignon only months before he died.

The performance in *Silent Night* takes place after a cosmic catastrophe.

> *Now then: here – on this stage:*
> *the end of the world*
> *after a disaster,*
> *a heap of dead bodies . . .*
> *and a heap of broken Objects –*
> *this is all that is left.*
>
> . . .
>
> *It all started,*
> *earlier, much earlier*
> *than the production discussed here*
> *An image of the end,*
> *of the end of life,*
> *of death,*
> *of calamity,*
> *of the end of the world,*
> *has always been deeply present*
> *in my imagination*
> *or maybe, it has been part of me.*

Kantor confesses that he had always been fascinated by the mythic Atlantis disaster, by "that 'world' before our world." The reference here is to Plato's νυξ χαλεπη, the "grievous night" of the destruction and disappearance of Atlantis in the depths of the ocean as the result of a violent earthquake.[26] In the cricotage, that night of death and annihilation is superimposed on – or invades – the peaceful night (*Stille Nacht*) of the birth of Christ. Death is a prerequisite for new life to appear. The End of the World is also the Birth of the World. From the perspective we have adopted here, the catastrophic event of "that night" that is repeated in this performance represents the "primal scene" as defined above and considered to be the root of all theater.

The characters on stage – Kantor reminds us – are all dead. They return "after that night" to repeat events that took place in the remotest past: births, crucifixions, decapitations, explosions, the end of the world, so new life can arise. There is hope that the repetition may differ from the "original" and allow us to see the "original" as if for the first time. We, the spectators, occupy an ambiguous bi-focal position, both before the original event and after, looking at its second edition as if for the first time, yet knowing that "we have already seen this!"[27] The repetition, however, fails; it leads to defeat ("the root of tragedy"). The figures have no recollection of the past – or, "everything is nothing more than a recollection":

> *Their attempts at putting*
> *the memory shreds together*
> *are futile and desperate.*

All is in vain as the past cannot be resuscitated.

Is this, finally, a closure? Kobialka[28] believes that *Silent Night* marked a shift in Kantor's theatrical practice in that "memory now invokes the un-representable in presentation itself." Kantor clearly struggles here to reach " the primordial layers of life" (*Milano Lessons, No. 6*) where birth and death are indistinguishable. *Silent Night* indicates the ultimate goal of Kantor's theater, indeed of all theater, which is to articulate the Un-representable. Brutally confronted with the "aporia of historical knowledge"[29] Kantor constructs a space that can receive the absence of representation, a space that can "present again" the un-representable pictogram and, by so doing, invest it with being (identity) and meaning so it can become part of the autobiographical record.[30] The *mise-en-scène* here is a *mettre-en-être* of the un-representable pre-symbolic event that can, now, "acquire its historical, philosophical and artistic function."[31] However, Kobialka's penetrating analysis points to the categorical tension between body and Logos and to the instability of the emerging pre-organic fragments that are engaged in a "strenuous search for the memory of the Other that coincides with the Self, who will always remain beyond it."[32]

This is the Kantor of 1990. His dead troupes returning, however, coming back to life "according to the principles of my theater," take us back to his 1944 Odysseus.

The mad theater of war infected Kantor's art and left its indelible mark on it. Wyspiański's *The Return of Odysseus* was performed by Kantor's Underground Theater in 1944 in a half-demolished room where reality, becoming indistinguishable from illusion, displaced it from view: he called this "intensified realism." In this foundationally deranged universe, where the dimensions of both place ("here" – "there") and time ("now" – "then") have collapsed, only something momentous can take place. The bent figure on stage, in rags, "a formless mass, merging with other objects in the room," its back turned to the spectator, remains silent. Suddenly, when the word "Troy" is heard, "a human face appears out of the formless mass." He turns his head to the audience and says this one sentence: "I am Odysseus" (*Theatrical Place*).[33]

This figure, the ghost of Odysseus that has returned from Troy/ Stalingrad in 1244 BCE[34]/1944 CE, became the *prototype* for all the later characters of Kantor's theater, as he tells us in *Theatrical Place*, and unquestionably contained the seeds for his Theater of Death.[35] Kantor explains that his work on the staging of *The Return of Odysseus* was driven by "a theoretical investigation into the nature of theatrical problems" (*Theatrical Place*).[36] He confesses that, already in his university years, he was attracted to

> the ominous subject-matter of *The Return of Odysseus, or, should I say, the despair and tragic impossibility of return to one's homeland.*
>
> (*Theatrical Place*)

So here we are, as we will be again forty-six years later in *Silent Night*, in a dilapidated room following a world catastrophe, in a room – or is it a cemetery? – populated by ghosts "appearing at the threshold between the shadow of death and life." Here, where "imagination materializes as reality" and "a mysterious current flows from the depth of time," a "miracle" (*Theatrical Place*) is about to happen: Odysseus – until now "No-Man" (Οὗτις)[37] – suddenly becomes "*une ombre parlante*"[38] assuming a name and an identity: "I am Odysseus," he asserts. This produces a strong, long-lasting emotion in the spectator, says Kantor. Why? We believe that the importance of this moment lies in representing the birth of the subject, the birth of the *I*, which can only occur when there is an overlap, a co-incidence between the individual's birth (Odysseus in his native land) and a calamitous deadly event (War of Troy), when there is a double conjunction of place (there is here) and of time (then is now). This happens when the word "Troy" is uttered. The recollection and retrieval of the disastrous event "here-and-now" links it directly to Odysseus' birthplace. "Troy" – like "That night" – represents the primordial violent event of origins. Only at the point of invocation of that catastrophic event, at the point of its recollection here in the native shores of the individual, in other words, only at the point in which the birth event and the death event coincide and coalesce, can the subject become an *I*, subject to time and to space (separateness). There has to be, first, a double collapse of both time (memory as ανα-μνησις, as re-actualization) and space (formless mass merged with surrounding objects) before linear time and *I – not-I* separation can be inaugurated, before the *I* can be born as an individual that is ek-static, i.e., continuously displaced by time (Heidegger[39]). This is a moment of existential shock. The *I* is born in ruins. True identity emerges when and if there is recognition of violence as constitutive of the self, indeed as giving birth to the self. "Troy" and "Ithaka," – the locus of disaster and nurturing haven – are twins, doubles or mirror images of each other, so that the true *I* is founded on a double vision, it is "binocular," as Bion would say.[40] When, by contrast, violence (the Death instinct) is located externally, as it is in the Homeric episode of Odysseus with the "monocular" Cyclops, Odysseus can only be a "No-Name."

Once linear time is affirmed, the *I* can become its own historian, constructing itself retro- and pro-actively. The integrated "binocular" *I* is, in the words of Heidegger, a "Being-towards-Death," a "whole" Dasein. It is an *I* that has integrated into its being the potentiality of non-being, or, rather, death as an actuality. This brings us back to Herakleitos the "obscure." Kantor speaks of the moment when a dead character has found his double, a living double[41] (*Theatrical Place*). This is an echo of Herakleitos' claim:

> *Immortal mortals, mortal immortals, these living the death of those, those dying the life of these.*

Kantor has understood – perhaps more than any other theater artist – that for the construction of true identity, or for theater to perform its true function, Odysseus *must* return (*Theatrical Place*). In his return, Odysseus brings phantasy (the primal scene) into the reality of the poor Room, transforms it into "real" and thereby provides the ground for authentic identity.

The imperative of return of the ghost of Odysseus, carrier of the memory of an ancient violence that always remains actual and defines us as individuals, led to Kantor's Theater of Death. There is a pressing need to link up with a primal wound situated in "that other world," to find a transition from the world of death to the world of the living and to name the un-namable. Odysseus traces the route of the return of the dead which all of Kantor's personages must take ("the stage is like a cemetery"). His ghost is a messenger of the other world, an underworld left behind and "forgotten." Odysseus becomes the "ford" in the river that Kantor had always been looking for, the passage that would allow the living to join up with their dead parts, the border zone that would make possible the meeting of doubles. So, Odysseus is the prototype of the actor, but he is also, the archetype of the artist. Art journeys along that ford that links the world "here" with the world "there," bringing back pale shadows of dead parts of the self, memories of a primal wound, the Real masked behind the illusory. Thus art, ultimately, labors in the service of true identity. However, Kantor's project is more ambitious. Abolishing the barrier, he wishes to return, re-unite with the dead parts and revive them. Yet he knows the "despair and tragic impossibility of return." No-one can cross Acheron twice. His project is not only revolutionary; it is blasphemous and hybristic. He seeks to create the world for a second time: an impossible task, as he eventually discovers (at the end of his life when he is no longer "at the border," but crosses it irreversibly). The construction of identity can only be a "work-in-progress," an aim never definitively reached – or reached only from the other side. Kantor's theater stages the possibility of the impossible.

It is in his 1975 Manifesto of *The Theater of Death*[42] that we find Kantor's most explicit statement of his conception of true theater. Art aims to reveal Being, to go behind appearances and expose the true nature of things that lies there hidden. Kantor, here, refers to Plato's search for the Real and describes his own search for it in the objects of everyday life, the "ready-made reality" of useless objects bereft of their life function, de-symbolized – indeed pre-symbolic – "objects of the Lowest Rank" between nothingness and eternity. The reality of appearances on which traditional theater is based must be pushed aside if theater is to maintain its art status. In this project of stripping apparent reality of its deceptive disguises (soothing though those may be) to get to the deeper truth, Kantor shares Freud's interests, as already mentioned, but his approach of gradually removing all the covering layers is urgent and free of any restraints. He wants to get down, or back, to the original Divine Marionette (Craig[43]) that harbors the secret of true theater: Death. In his stripping away of all the protective human defenses, Kantor audaciously goes un-hesitantly to the extreme, directly to the *absence of life*, to Freud's *Todestrieb*: "the concept of LIFE can be vindicated in art only through the ABSENCE OF LIFE," he insists. This journey is, of course, antithetical to life and represents a transgression, i.e., a rebellious disregard of boundaries. So, the MANNEQUIN, Kantor's Actor, makes his appearance:

> . . . *a manifestation of the Dark, Nocturnal, Rebellious side of human activity. Of Crimes and Traces of Death as sources of recognition . . . transmitting to us a terrifying message of Death and Nothingness.*[44]

In a manner that strikingly echoes Aristotle's theory of the origins of tragedy, Kantor "ascribes a History" to the course of events that led to the birth of the Actor and the birth of Theater. As in the old theory of the birth of tragedy out of a ritual assembly, he tells us, there came a time when "SOMEONE" took the risk of breaking off from the ritualistic community. This "act of SEVERANCE (RUPTURE)" was a "tragic act daring to remain alone with Fate," and carried a "MESSAGE of extraordinary import." The situation that eventually resulted was a face-to-face encounter between two beings that looked alike but were *different* in a fundamental way, two selves, the Other being "infinitely DISTANT, shockingly FOREIGN as if DEAD" and anchored on the other side of an invisible barrier. This was a traumatic moment bringing about a "metaphysical shock," an uncanny moment[45] in which something familiar but long forgotten re-appears, "as if they [those who remained within the ritual circle] had seen him [the Other] FOR THE FIRST TIME, as if they had seen THEIR VERY SELVES." This is the experience that inhabits our dreams or nightmares, Kantor adds. However, even behind that – we might add – this is the stuff of our primal phantasies. The moment is "uncanny" because, although it is encountered as if for the first time, it has been lived through before, at the very origins of our being. Kantor sees in this unsettling experience the emergence of tragic consciousness "measuring its FATE on an inexorable and final scale, the *scale* of DEATH." Time, in other words, linear time, establishes its relentless sovereignty. For Kantor, theater must recover the shock of this primeval force.

We recognize in the experience that Kantor describes here the derivatives of the indelible contents of a deeply buried phantasy of a traumatic primal scene: that of the birth of individual consciousness, of the birth of the *I*, out of a split fusional bodily matrix. As we have suggested, this is the scene that lies at the root not only of tragedy but of theater as a whole. A theater such as Kantor's that deals with the very nature of theater cannot but zoom into these primordial events. This is a theater which, like psychoanalysis, seeks to transgress the "impassable BARRIER" – risky and disturbing though this action may be – and bring us face-to-face with "the tragic and menacing beauty of Death." This *aenigmatic* (in the Aristotelian sense) and horrifying beauty is the ultimate paradox of the human condition. However, the impossible task now facing us is the compelling need to establish a *relation* between the two domains of human consciousness, to construct a link between the two distinct parts of the self. Kantor recognizes that only through object relations can we construct meaning and render the incomprehensible tolerable and the *aenigmatic* innocuous. The challenge, however, is daunting since it calls for a trans-categorical linkage.

The method that Kantor develops to "materialize" his vision of a theater that recovers the "primeval shock" is based on his use of space and is organically centered on the DOOR. His stage, his ROOM, is invaded by the objects – dead objects, ghosts – that inhabit the dark, crowded space *behind* the stage. Those figures seem pressured to come out through the DOOR that links the visible world with the invisible. The wall that separates them is weak (*The Room: Maybe a New Phase*). Kantor's stage is, in fact, the space behind the door, Freud's *Andere Platz*, the primal Unconscious pushing to come out. It is Anna O.'s "room of imagination," the stage of her "private theater." Kantor describes this "INTERIOR" space that contains the UR-MATTER of theater "as a battlefield, as a volcano," an "INFERNO – a constant MOTION" (*My Work – My Journey*).[46]

> . . . *doors . . . open suddenly to*
> *the deeper and deeper regions of what might otherwise be seen as a domestic Interior.*
> *Inside, in a suffocating and humid atmosphere, the dreams are unfolded, the nightmares are born,*
> *behaviors which hate the light of day are practiced . . .*
>
> (A Wardrobe)[47]

> *Important events stand behind the doors*
> *it is enough to open them . . .*
>   (*The Room: Maybe a New Phase*)[48]

> *Disclosing it . . . has an almost metaphysical and sacred quality.*
> (Theatrical Place)[49]

This concealed space clearly overlaps with the Freudian Unconscious, a buried world in which reason and the laws of logic are unknown. It is a world that interfaces with the Un-representable, the un-symbolizable Void, Freud's "navel." Beyond it – says Kantor – there is Nothing, which explains the meta-physical awe and horror evoked by this obscure universe.

At the door, ghosts – those beings from another dimension, from "regions that are inaccessible to our minds," equivocal creatures (Schulz[50]) – are impatiently waiting to make their grand entrance. The stage we now see is a cemetery. It is a womb-tomb "giving birth to something new and unexpected" (*Theatrical Place*). The door is the ford in the river, the passage that permits the communication of this world with the "other side." It is itself a testament and testimony of the traumatic schism, a concretization and affirmation of an irreversibly divided reality. Further, there is someone – a ubiquitous lean figure in dark clothes and an intense look – that beckons us "at the threshold" of this Gate, an anti-Charon conducting the *return* of the dead.

Death in Greek tragedy resides exclusively in the invisible space behind the *skene*. It could not be otherwise in Kantor's stage, or in Freud's Unconscious (death drive): behind Kantor's Door, there is the realm of Death. Yet, concealed, or repressed, "this is where the threads of our memory are woven" (*The Room: Maybe a New Phase*). Memory, through its untamable and illogical meanders, leads to that which is memory only because it is "forgotten." However, it is the "forgotten" that is the Real – a conviction that runs uninterrupted from Plato (*Meno*), through Freud, to Kantor. In this interior Room the memory of "That night" is preserved in all its fragments, shrouded and buried, but alive. This is the *Ur-szene* of birth and of death, of eternity and nothingness, of the *primal loss*. "We have to accept memory as the only realness" (*Theatrical Place*), as an immaterial memory of physical, bodily transmuting states and events.

The ghost – Kantor's actor – constructed out of the threads of memory, enters uninvited (?) through the Door into our Room during a *séance* – or is it a ritual? He is a Messenger of the Other World, allowing us to have an obscured glimpse into the Dark Universe since the River cannot be crossed twice. Unlike Freud's dream, the Messenger is not the "royal road" that would guide us *back* to the Other World. Instead, the Messenger carries shreds, impressions, odors of the Other World *to* us, but even though he can name himself, the Messenger cannot name the un-nameable.

Kantor's arrangement of a "meta-physical" theatrical space makes this space analogous to Freud's meta-psychological psychic space. There is, first, the room of deceptive appearances (illusions). Then there is a barrier, and behind it there is the room of deeper concealed truths (psychic reality, unconscious phantasies). Finally, there is the incomprehensible, unknowable "navel" – the Void. Primordial forces of Eros and Thanatos inhabit the Room of psychic reality. We consider that Kantor's ghost/actors, dead objects that nevertheless remain alive, are derivatives of dead parts of the self following the rupture, division and fragmentation of the original psychosomatic matrix (One), an event encoded in a "primal scene." The *I* is constituted of these fragments and the *I* is a carrier of death.

Notes

1 *Sema* = tombstone.
2 "Poland has not perished yet" (Polish national anthem).
3 Wyspiański's stained glass window, in Pawilon Wyspiański 2000, Kraków.

4 R. Martinis, *Tadeusz Kantor – CRICOT 2* (Salerno / Milano: Oedipus edizioni, 2001), 16.
5 J. Chrobak, L. Stangret and M. Świca, *Tadeusz Kantor Wędrówka* (Kraków: Cricoteka, 2000).
6 T. Kantor, *The Milano Lessons, No. 12*, in *A Journey Through Other Spaces*, ed. and trans. M. Kobialka (Berkeley: U. of California P., 1993), 205–265.
7 T. Kantor, *Métamorphoses* (Paris: Hachette, 1982), 95. Translation by the author.
8 M. Romanska, *The Post-traumatic Theater of Grotowski and Kantor* (London: Anthem Press, 2012).
9 M. Kobialka, *Further On Nothing* (Minneapolis: U. of Minnesota P., 2009), 444.
10 A. Halczak, *Teatr Cricot 2 Informator 1989–1990* (Kraków: Cricoteka, 1991), 184.
11 Kobialka (2009), 411.
12 *Ibid.*, 404.
13 *Ibid.*, 441.
14 Kobialka (1993), 247.
15 Kobialka, (2009), 352.
16 *Ibid.*, 350.
17 *Ibid.*, 208.
18 Guide to the performance of *Let the Artists Die*. Translated by the author.
19 M. Kobialka (2009), 237.
20 *Wielopole, Wielopole, Partytura*, in M. Kobialka (2009), 291.
21 Kobialka (2009), 353.
22 *Milano Lessons, No. 11*, in M. Kobialka (1993), 245.
23 In M. Kobialka (2009), 386.
24 *Milano Lessons, No. 6*, in M. Kobialka (1993), 234.
25 Kobialka (2009), 434–457.
26 Plato (1973), *Timaeus*, 25d.
27 cf. D. W. Winnicott, "Fear of breakdown," *Int. Rev. Psycho-Anal.*, 1974: 103.
28 Kobialka (2009), 416.
29 *Ibid.*, 428.
30 Aulagnier (1975).
31 *Milano Lesson No. 1*, in Kobialka (1993), 212.
32 M. Kobialka (2009), 429.
33 *Ibid.* 352.
34 Fictitious date.
35 It should be noted that Kantor's father went to war (WWI), but never returned and was presumed dead – until Kantor, in his twenties, met him once accidentally. In 1942, the family received an official letter informing them that Marian Kantor had "died of a heart attack" at Auschwitz. In the Guide of *I Shall Never Return* we hear Marian's voice saying: "I died on the 24th January 1944." Odysseus is clearly linked with Kantor's father ("I was waiting anxiously and faithfully for the return of Odysseus") who returns from the war dead.
36 Kobialka (2009), 329.
37 *Odyssey*, 9: 364.
38 Aulagnier (1975), 136.
39 M. Heidegger, *Being and Time* (New York: Harper Collins, 1962).
40 Bion, (1984), 14.
41 Kobialka (2009), 350.

42 T. Kantor, "The theater of death," *TDR*, 1975: 137–148.
43 E.G. Craig, *On the Art of the Theater* (New York: Theater Art Books, 1956), 54–94.
44 Kantor (1975), 143.
45 Freud, *S.E.* 17: 217–256.
46 Kobialka (2009), 4–5.
47 *Ibid.*, 64.
48 *Ibid.*, 369.
49 *Ibid.*, 339.
50 B. Schulz, *Les boutiques de cannelle* (Paris: Denoël, 1974), 75.

6   Personal confessions

Although Kantor considered his four plays, *The Dead Class, Wielopole, Wielopole, Let the Artists Die* and *I Shall Never Return*, as his "personal confessions," all of his theater must be seen as the most intimate anguished confession of a true artist. He offered himself as a mirror to his spectators, "*Ecce homo*":

> *I am . . . on stage*
> *I will not be a performer.*
> *Instead, poor fragments of my*
> *own life*
> *will become*
> *"ready-made objects."*
>
> *Every night*
> *RITUAL*
> *And SACRIFICE*
> *will be performed here.*
>   *(To Save from Oblivion)*[1]

His is an intimate theater of an irreparable loss, never comprehended, never accepted. Memory betrays, never fills the gap. Mourning is interminable. The spirits of the dead (dead fragments of the self) are invoked in a séance, but only to return to their shadowy existence in the crypt behind the door. Each production is a *danse macabre*, a ritual of death, a re-play of a "primal murder," the human tragedy brought into poignant relief by the burlesque. Sophokles' words endlessly reverberate in the thick walls of the underground Galeria Krzysztofory:

Αιδα φευξιν ουκ επαξεται.[2]

Aenigma

The parcours to *The Dead Class* was long and tortuous, but Kantor regarded his Theater of Death as a direct continuation of his 1963 "Zero Theater."[3] It is, perhaps, worth noting that in 1962 Kantor's mother, Helka, died. There followed a "turning point" for Kantor, according to Pleśniarowicz.[4] This had been a time of preoccupation with a descent into Hades and, in the previous year, Kantor had written an essay entitled *Is the Return of Orpheus Possible?* In 1963 he staged Witkiewicz' *The Madman and the Nun*, which marked the appearance of his short-lived Zero Theater. In this play, an attempted dialogue between a Madman and a Nun turns into absurdity as the message cannot pass through an intervening barrier (the "two informers") without being distorted. A huge pyramidal "Machine of Annihilation" dominated the stage. Meaning was, thus, reduced to zero. In the following year, Kantor discovers his *ambalaze*. He passionately packaged and wrapped up everything in envelopes, sacks, parcels, bags, but also in clothes that seemed to contain a human figure. This "human *emballage*" suggesting a shroud was a more explicit expression of the artist's intention to *preserve an object* and protect it from decay. These were "pathetic remains of greatness," he says, "between garbage and eternity." The object, now invisible, continues to carry on a secret existence deep inside its secure shelter forever. Zero Theater and *emballages* eventually led to the Theater of Death.

The psychoanalyst is apt to see, perhaps, too many personal themes in this crucial phase in the development of Kantor's art following his mother's death, but it may not be an exaggeration to suspect a relation of these events to old and profound feelings of loss that were now rekindled in Kantor's inner world. For him, the dead never stopped living in their graves (*Silent Night*): Marian, Odysseus, Eurydice, Helka? However, the need to communicate with them is, of necessity, frustrated by a stubborn barrier that blocks re-union.

The Dead Class, the first play of the trilogy of Kantor's Theater of Death, is a dream or a hallucination. It might have been a nightmare if Kantor's "human meta-physics"[5] hadn't intervened. However, his delicate balancing on a tightrope between the pathetic and the grotesque accentuates only too painfully the tragic. Unquestionably, his is a theater of emotions. Apparitions, spectral figures, emerge through a dark opening recalling Homer's *eidola* begging to be buried and forgotten so they can find peace. They come from "the other side," the Underworld, or the deep Unconscious:

> *The stage action consists of a chain of sequences which do not form a logical plot, are not logically connected; each one of them is its own beginning, they are isolated and exist for themselves. Moreover, the fact that they are "close to each other" is shocking and absurd.*
>
> (*The Dead Class, Director's Notebook*)[6]

The irrational, haphazard and loose associations among these freely mobile unconscious elements create a disquieting tension that moves the action forward by doubling it upon itself.

To sequentially describe the various dis-jointed events of *The Dead Class* unfolding in front of the spectator's eyes offers little to the reader. Worse, it betrays the spirit of the piece. This is a powerful visual and auditory intimate emotional experience that cannot be put in the rational language of prose. Kantor calls it a séance. Following the logic of the Unconscious, it resembles a psychotic universe, nonetheless uncannily familiar. Alien, yet melancholy and painfully nostalgic. This parallel surreal world echoes the work of three authors dear to Kantor: Bruno Schulz, Stanislaw Witkiewicz and Witold Gombrowicz. The idea of old men returning to their schoolroom and re-living the memories of their schooldays comes from Schulz' short story, *The Pensioner*[7] read through the lens of Gombrowicz' mocking irony. The fragmentary text they speak in a dislocated, incoherent manner comes from Witkiewicz' *Tumor Mózgowicz* (*Tumor Brainard*). However, it "would be unjustified bibliophilic pedantry," Kantor notes, "to attempt to find those missing fragments necessary for a complete 'knowledge' of the plot of this play."[8]

The spectator enters the space of an old decrepit classroom:

> *From the last forgotten shred of our memory, somewhere in a strait corner, there project a few rows of poor wooden school BENCHES . . .*
> *dessicated BOOKS disintegrate into dust . . .*[9]

The pupils, old dotards on the edge of the grave, make their *grande entrée* carrying real sized puppets of small children,

> *like little corpses . . .*
> *some of these are swaying inertly, clinging with a desperate movement, hanging, trailing, as if they were the remorse of conscience, curling up at the actors' feet, as if creeping over these metamorphosed specimens . . . human creatures unashamedly exhibiting the secrets of their past. . . with the EXCRESCENCES of their own CHILDHOOD . . .*[10]

The old men–pupils take their places on the benches, shuffle around in an agitated fashion, make silly jokes and pranks, torment each other, run to the Loo, collapse to the ground, endlessly repeating the same actions. There is, notably, THE WOMAN IN A WINDOW anxiously and helplessly trying to convey something urgent, something of the world on the other side of the glass. There is AN OLD MAN IN THE LOO, AN OLD MAN WITH THE BICYCLE constantly riding around carrying a dead child with his arms outstretched, A SOMNAMBULISTIC PROSTITUTE exposing her breasts with obscene gestures, a BEADLE "into whom has flowed all the melancholy of time past," A WOMAN WITH A MECHANICAL CRADLE or coffin, giving birth to two wooden balls, and, most importantly, the Leader of the Chorus, as it were, the CHARWOMAN-DEATH with her broom/scythe. There are other characters, equally distinct and ambiguous, but there is, also, the Conductor of this cacophonous bizarre universe, Kantor himself on stage. The sequence, structure and even inclusion of each of the various disconnected episodes composing the stage action would change from one performance to another. At the center of it all, there is a funerary ceremony, an All Souls Day: Kantor's GREAT GAME WITH THE VOID.

If *aenigma* is an impossible linkage, it is evident that aenigmatic "objects" and actions populate Kantor's stage. The BIO-OBJECT – this peculiar amalgam of a living body with its excrescences – is, like the Sphinx, *itself* a riddle. The Sphinx's question to Oedipus concerned the identity of man. Similarly, the BIO-OBJECT poses the question of man's paradoxical identity. Like the Sphinx who pronounces a riddle by *being* it, so does the BIO-OBJECT, which is, really, a BIO-THANATO-OBJECT. Here is the impossible (incomprehensible) combinatory nature of the *aenigma*. Horrifying and fascinating (cf. Kristeva's *abject*), it draws us into its time-less Dance of Death. The BIO-THANATO-OBJECT poses the question of man's identity by positing Time and its riddles.

Kantor recalls the birth of this idea in his *Director's Notebook*:

> *I call it the MAIN IDEA.*
> *The basis of the whole performance.*
> *On one lucky day an idea occurs to me that I might join together the actors,*
>   *old people, returning to their former classroom where they are expecting to*
>   *catch their childhood memories, with the wax figures of children dressed in*
>   *school uniforms – join them literally and for good.*

However, these are corpses of children in a mortuary, children that have been murdered. Kantor calls this the Massacre of the Innocents. "The old people carry them, their own childhoods . . . a monstrous ANTHROPOLOGICAL SPECIMEN." Equivocal beings, it is never clear whether they return pleading to be buried so they can find peace, as in Homer, or whether they keep coming back wanting to come alive again ("the performance means a new life to them," we read in the *Director's Notebook*). The dead children clinging desperately to the old men are dead parts, fragments of the old men's selves that refuse to be left behind after a "catastrophe" dictated by Nature's laws, the laws that lay down the conditions for being, (in our sense: the "primal scene"). This strange "anthropological specimen" is a hybrid living dead object that carries in its very substance the dead matter of its origins, its double. In so doing it is charged with a living tension and possesses a capacity to communicate in signs, but not in symbols. It communicates to us – albeit in a dysarthric way – the incomprehensible in human identity. In its status of a liminal creature, the BIO-OBJECT is a Messenger of the Real. It is composed of the two un-integrated constituents of the *I*, two fragments imprisoned in the same body and condemned to need and oppose each other forever. The dead matter continues to live parasitically on the living flesh and conversely. As time is collapsed, the material body of the actor/mannequin bears indelibly inscribed on it the death of its primordial beginning and that of its ultimate end. The BIO-OBJECT – an eternal, irreducible duality – is a monument of the ontological schism of origins, a memory record of that event. *The Dead Class* is, thus, a dream that records an ancient memory; it is not a concocted fantasy but a (pre) historical document dug out of the yellow pages of the self's shredded archives scattered on the ground. Oneiric images are embodied in the BIO-OBJECTS that re-live nebulous pre-memory states of an irretrievable archaic past in a disintegrating post-memory present. As a biform self, the BIO-OBJECT is Kantor's double, but in Kantor's theater the BIO-OBJECT *par excellence* is "*Kantor-with-his-stage.*" It is this uncanny coupling that generates all the psychic energy and tension of his theater.

The nature of this primordial binary unit, the BIO-OBJECT – two unassimilated fragments of the self brought together – is reflected in its peculiar "language." This is a language that expresses fragmentation. When it exhibits a rudimentary structure, it carries no meaning; it is a foreign language that remains on the surface of the object, never entering its substance, never becoming part of it. The object "plays" with it – is even fascinated by it – as a child would play with a toy. Kantor places a strong emphasis on language in *The Dead Class*. He disintegrates the structure of language to reach down to Winnicott's state of "un-integration."

> *I attempted to break the . . . literary reality of the dramatic text with ANOTHER REALITY.*
>
> (*The Dead Class*, Director's Notebook)

The "other reality" – when it is not broken up and chaotic – speaks a proto-linguistic language which is, thoroughly, a language of the body. It follows its own grammatical rules, or, rather, follows no rules at all. It lacks syntactic, or even phonetic structure, preserving only the primitive rhythm that is anchored in the functioning of the body and echoes archaic body states (cf. Aulagnier's *pictogrammes*). Rhythmic repetitiveness is expressed in echolalia. Language ends up being a flood of inarticulate sounds, meaningless phonemes, gibberish, a language that is "finally reduced to groans." Groan as a cry is, of course, the first utterance of the body, the first breath (*psychein*), so groan is the archaic language of the psyche preserved in its depths. Language there is a-symbolic, or, rather, pre-symbolic. It is a "thing-language," where the word is an autonomous physical object that executes a material act; it carries no symbolic link to an object other than itself. Not only the objects' verbal utterances *per se*, but the whole "language" of the production is situated in fact – as is always the case with Kantor – in an area at the border between sign and symbol. This is the area of what Hanna Segal calls "symbolic equations."[11] A symbolic equation makes no distinction between the thing and the word. The word *is* the thing, rather than "standing for" the thing: "heel" *is* the anatomical heel, and so is "finger" and "Cleopatra's nose." In not distinguishing between thing and word, symbolic equations belong to a world before the integration of the subject (the *I*) into a "whole subject" that is separate from the object.

In search of that proto-language, Kantor paid particular attention to the language of children, when they begin to speak. They struggle to give expression to the contents of their "subconscious," he says,

> *lacking connective expressions, prepositions, conjunctions that might give sentences their direction, meaning and sense . . . a desperate search for the forgotten fragment somewhere deep in memory, blanks, gaps that one wants to fill desperately and at all costs.*
>
> (*The Dead Class, Director's Notebook*)

The fragmented, disintegrated language of some psychotics points even more clearly to the struggle to verbalize the body's primitive states. Language, here, serves the purpose of an urgent discharge of energy released as the result of a disorganizing inner catastrophe and it bears the scars of that event.

The difficulty, the "barrier," between the body and the word/symbol, derives from their categorical difference, their non-isomorphism. They collide:

> *two realities indifferent to each other clash; a battle is fought whose rules and strategies do not hold a promise of victory to either party . . . all this looks like a battle fought by children or madmen.*
>
> (*The Dead Class*, Director's Notebook)

Language, being foreign to the body, is radically inadequate (cf. the *inadaequatio rei et intellectus* of the Scholastics) to express it. The collision between the two realities manifests the discord between Kantor's Ur-Matter and symbolic thought or reason authorized by the socius. The only possible resolution of this conflict is a parallel existence of two autonomous entities journeying side by side along a "two-track" path. Their autonomy even allows them to "play" with each other. However, there is no sign of bridging their irreconcilable differences; they remain utterly dis-jointed. Thus, the BIO-OBJECT in *The Dead Class* speaks words that belong to someone else. The Old Man in the Lavatory, for example,

> *repeats them without proper comprehension, he easily forgets about them and then again utters them unscrupulously with artificial euphoria and pathos . . .*
>
> (*The Dead Class*, Director's Notebook)

The gap between the two parallel worlds echoes the incongruous co-existence of the two unassimilated constituents of the BIO-OBJECT. However, significantly, the very existence of a gap between action and word, between "then" and "now," points to the operation of a primal violence as the origin of the fissure: the "primal scene." And it is this violence that is at the heart of *The Dead Class*.

The scene that portrays this foundational violence most poignantly is the cradle/coffin sequence: "birth and death – two mutually explainable arrangements." It is a scene that, as if in a dream, gives us a glimpse – a "privilege" Kantor calls it – "of seeing this life here from the other side that is inaccessible to our understanding." The scene is a ritual, "a primeval and, at the same time, a final ritual." The Woman lies on a gynecological table, her legs spread apart, about to give birth. She is excited and filled with joy:

> *I could just, out of sheer happiness, burst into pieces and turn into some magma of another world.*

A cradle is brought in by the repugnant CHARWOMAN-DEATH for the two newborns. However, the cradle looks like a little coffin for children, and the newborns turn out to be two dried-up wooden balls. As the Charwoman makes their cradle rock, a nightmarish clicking sound is produced by the balls hitting the side walls of the cradle, a beat that continues monotonously almost to the end. This is not a baby's cry. The rattling dried-up balls – heartbeats of the dead – will soon click in tandem with the deadly wide-sweeping movements of the Charwoman's metal broom/scythe that levels everyone to the ground. The wooden balls, Kantor says, are a "mystical image . . . of a baby reduced to a dead object, put to death, mutilated" (*Director's Notebook*). The usual washing of the newborn is replaced in this scene by the Charwoman's washing of corpses in this delivery room-turned-mortuary: she scrubs their faces, bellies, buttocks, groins meticulously, while the rhythmic clicking continues. The balls will be buried in the end, while the Prostitute stammers broken mutilated sentences about "an embryo . . ., in a sha . . ., sweet little . . .there was once . . ." Speech is clearly inadequate to describe or name this archaic event of the inextricable merging of birth and death. The lullaby sung by the Woman at the end – the monotonous rhythmic clatter continues – is both a cradlesong and a lament/Kaddish for the "sweet little baby" cast to the shadows. There is rage in the Woman's voice – no clowning here.

The incomprehensible mixture of living and dying is enacted again in the Outing scene. The sarcastic, cynical Death figure on the "other side of the glass," invites the children to go for a picnic on the hills:

> *Spring is in the air*
> *Catkins turn green on trees.*
> *I have seen two brimstone butterflies*
> *awakened by the warmth of the day*
> *ready to leave their larvae.*
> *They don't know, poor little darlings,*
> *they won't have any flowers to feed on yet*
> *and are bound to die . . .*

They all rush out beaming with joy. Soon, however, the scene turns into an anguished rush to death. "This is no longer a spring stroll, but a murderous run." The children/old men stumble, trip, fall to the ground. As the nostalgic waltz "François" is played in the background ("*If only the old days were back!*"), this mad agitated movement turns into a ghastly Dance of Death. Spring lilies and dead larvae, not juxtaposed, but completely overlapping: the *aenigma*.

The trauma of the primal scene of birth as a deathly rupture of a paradisiacal One-ness threatens to throw the organism into a prior state of un-integration, of chaos, of the Un-representable. This seems to be happening in the "Simultaneous Orgy" scene. The external action has now moved far away to a Pacific island, a savage world ruled by a volcano deity. The characters are transformed by some unknown illness; they are ravaged, wrecked. "We have crossed the threshold of sense and logic," Kantor writes in his *Notebook*. There is total confusion, hell, total disintegration, meaninglessness and aimlessness. The ruling God here seems to be a chaotic Power, that we would call EROTHANATOS. There is necrophilic debauchery, "from the cemetery to an orgy, from a grave to a brothel . . . a funebrial onanism." No distinction between the sacred and the vulgar, the putrid, the obscene. "Spasmodic shouting of raving desires and animal instincts" are both expressions of ecstasy and, at the same time, anguished groans of death. Pleasure is indistinguishable from pain. The All has merged with Nothing. Decaying corpses, dead penises, sperm and rot. This markedly erotic atmosphere carries an odor of death and decomposition. We end up with a tangle of "relics, victims of a funereal and orgiastic ritual." Their language is an unspeakable grunt that Kantor calls, teasingly, "a graphomaniac verse":

vzgζdδngiel
vzgζdδηha
vzgζdgrùha
vzgζdhiζda
. . .

All this seems to be what follows "That night," the night of the End of the World. This can lead nowhere, "is directed *towards nowhere*," as Kantor underlines in his *Notebook*.

The "nameless dread" of falling back into the chaos of un-integration is a permanent feature of the humid space of that classroom. A means of stopping the tide of regress is repetition. Repetition plays a most important role in Kantor's theater. It is his characteristic way of "playing with time," as he "plays with the Void." Repetition is, of course, the repetition of an original event – ultimately, in our sense, of the "primal scene" – but Kantor plays with repetitions of the repetition, and this also extends to the repetition in a given production of objects, figures and events that had appeared in other productions. A trauma calls for defensive ways of dealing with it, bringing into play various efforts to master it. Freud drew attention to individuals who, defensively, repeat rather than remember.[12] The trauma we are focusing on here is that of the original fragmentation and loss. The need is to re-capture the lost object, which is, really, a lost part of the self. Memory brings back the lost object, makes it present again. So does theater's *re-présentation*. However, memory turns out to be deceptive and murderous. The camera/machine gun held by the formidable Charwoman executes every object it turns its lens on. It doesn't bring it back. Memory is an instrument of death. It affirms and consolidates the unbearable loss. It doesn't *recall* the violent loss; it instantly *becomes* it, it *is* that violence. Moreover, if the loss is irreversible and intolerable, there is no other resort than to turn to endless compulsive repetitions intent on undoing the loss and bringing back the precious object. For Kantor, "REPETITION is both a protest and a challenge." His tormented objects "continue dropping dead and rising one by one for ever and ever" (*Illusion and Repetition*).[13] *The Dead Class* ends, but Kantor specifies:

> *And from now on they will continue to repeat their own words and gestures which are growing ever more empty and meaningless . . .*

The nostalgic need to reverse time and re-gain a lost paradise where the object can be re-united with its double leads to a stubborn attempt to annul time, or to create a repetitive *circular* time that erases and replaces relentless linear time and allows the return of what is lost (cf. Nietzsche's "eternal return"). This, however, leads to an interminable re-living of the trauma, a *re-présentation* of the pain. Kantor specifies that repetition is "a signal of SHRINKING TIME" (*Memory*).[14] As a result, "theatre always asserts itself in the present . . . This is what makes it so disturbing," Brook explains.[15] The conjoined birth scene and death scene of the primal trauma are collated so death is *now* and the pain is actual. The compulsion to repeat precludes psychic evolution and works in the service of the death drive.[16] The objects return, but only to disappear again going through the Door of Death. The effort to re-vitalize them is frustrated and repeated attempts fail. So, they are brought back again from the recesses of memory, they make their entry again in the dream, in a stubborn journey that reverses time. "Odysseus *must* return." There is a desperate struggle here to deny the loss, the irreparable break, to remove the barrier that permanently separates the living from the dead so the dead would be free to continue coming back. The dead never die. This means that mourning is impossible. Further, as the dead can never be laid to rest, mourning is endless.

The mourner, however, seems to have devised a secret scheme to hold on to his precious object – precious because it is part of his own self, a "selfobject." Kantor writes in his *Notebook*:

> *Everyone keeps repeating their halting gestures and words, which will never be completed, as if shackled and imprisoned by them forever.*

Here is the secret then: the object is trapped and kept prisoner in a half-living, half-dead state, shackled so it can never leave for good, it can never be lost. The mourner carries a "prison" within himself which is, really, a cemetery. The mourner (Kantor, or the spectator) is himself a BIO-THANATO-OBJECT wandering aimlessly in the eternity of arrested time, a BIO-THANATO-OBJECT, or a human EMBALLAGE-SHROUD striving "to preserve and to escape the passage of time." Kantor's prison is, thus, endowed with special characteristics that can transform it into a space of freedom and creativity. These, Kantor confesses, are "the ontological aspects of prison and its . . . eschatology" (*Prison*).[17]

The "prison guard" whom we see on stage, "at the threshold" of the prison door, is a peculiar, a paradoxical kind of guard. His mission is to free the prisoners, to let them out of the jail they have been condemned to. So he admits that his presence there is "illegal." In an interview with Anne Ubersfeld[18] Kantor explains that he is present on stage in order to destroy illusion, to eliminate fiction. He wants to provoke the public, he says, by revealing what is conventionally hidden, referring to the fact that, as a director, he is, of course expected *not* to be on stage. Kantor's wish to reveal what is normally hidden by putting himself on stage expresses his belief that through the presence of his own "Real *I*" he can best expose the hidden truth and give us a glimpse into "the other side"; what resides *behind* the visible:

> To enter the stage,
> not as a "guardian" of a fortress,
> which I defended against "performing,"
> but as a real "I"
> (The Real "I")[19]

Kantor on the stage of *The Dead Class* is, really, the dreamer of his dream. What troubles, what startles the spectator, is precisely that stark juxtaposition of the dreamer and his dream; specifically, the gap between the dreaming *I* and the dreamed *I*. Hypnos, *Thanatos*, brothers, the offspring of Night: the shock comes from the unsettling encounter of the living with the dead. Kantor's presence on stage highlights the gap, punctuates the division within the substance of the *I*. The *I* is fragmented into a present part-*I* and another part left behind, a dead *I*, the result of an original rupture following a mythic catastrophe. Identity is tragically and irreversibly fragmented. This makes Kantor the BIO-THANATO-OBJECT *par excellence*, as has been mentioned: Kantor-cum-his-dead-ghost actors. A Kantor on stage struggles, in vain, to mediate between the two, to control the madness (see, e.g., the scene of Automata), but there is also the illicit Kantor who incites the madness, stresses the tragic rift. The tension that results from the confrontation of the radically alienated dis-joined ingredients of his ego is the source of the magic of his art.

So, what we see on stage are the dispersed fragments of a self, *"poor fragments of* my life . . . *ready-made objects"* and

> *Every night*
> *RITUAL*
> *and SACRIFICE*
> *will be performed here.*
>   *(To Save from*
>   *Oblivion)*[20]

Every night a ritual of repetition that repeats an ancient trauma and re-affirms the unbridgeable gap as it strives to eliminate it.

The Dead Class is Kantor's major statement of the conditions of human inner reality. It is an exposition as well as *une exposition* of the inner land-scape in all its breadth. It served as the basis on which he could proceed to develop the project of his "personal confessions." It was a "discovery" that had been preceded by a long preparatory step-by-step research. The guiding principle, however, had been clearly and emphatically enunci-ated from the very beginning. This was The Return:

> *Some great mystery of life*
> *Lies in this magical word: RETURN.*
> *The human yearning for RETURN.*
>   *(The Return)*[21]

There is, undoubtedly, a whole meta-physical theory behind this *Weltanschauung*, and, definitely, a meta-psychological one. The meta-psychological theory – best articulated by the Kleinians and Winnicott – places *loss* at the center of all human endeavor. "Return" means a strong desire for the *return of* a lost object that is felt as vital to the self, but it also means a profound wish to *return to* a former state of serenity and absence of all tension. The different emphasis on either of these two senses of "return" defines essential differences between the Kleinian and the Freudian schools. However, both theories would agree that a strong, inflexible, uncompromising, compulsive need of *return*, in either of the two senses, is an indication of the dominance of a destructive drive, the death drive. The task of life, then, would be to mitigate this need. Which raises the question: Does theater work in the service of life, specifically, as an activity that strives to deal with issues of loss, schism, integration, tol-eration of fragmentation and incompleteness and endeavors to promote the construction of meaning and identity?

The Dead Class does not aim to make advances in this direction. Rather, it "exhibits" the state of affairs, as it were, the "State of Dis-union." At the end of the *séance*, we, the spectators, we, who have been "waiting for the actors," must create linear time. Is Kantor going to help us in this?

What those who have returned have shown us were broken images, fragments of a meaningless existence, shadows of lifeless prisoners of an eternally revolving yet static universe, grotesque, enigmatic, incongruous combinations of unassimilated bits of being, ontologic divisions, unbridgeable gaps, disintegrations into a chaotic magma, nostalgia for a paradise lost – endless mourning.

This uncanny, frightful, even unlivable experience must be put into some sort of a "container" (Bion) to be tolerated. Our grand scientific theories are, perhaps, no more than that. The specific schema suggested here reduces this nightmare into the dream of a phantasy. We claim that this dream derives from – or "screens"[22] – a phantasy of a primordial catastrophic originary event (the "primal scene") that was simultaneously birth and death, an archaic event that took place in a pre-temporal, pre-mental past and left its indelible trace in the Unconscious. This would explain its persistent Return.

Shady individuals

Wielopole, Wielopole came five years after *The Dead Class*. The focus here is directly on the mechanism of memory. In its specificity, it could almost be considered as a theatrical treatise on the epistemology of memory. However, it is also, more than any other play, Kantor's "private theater."[23] The various themes and events in this private theater unfold – as with *The Dead Class* – within the space-time frame of a dream. However, this dream is a special kind of a dream; it is a dream-as-memory. Psychoanalytic practice has drawn attention to a particular category of dreams that are not the product of condensation and displacement of repressed elements in the unconscious now resurfacing, but rather the return of forgotten events accompanied by concrete details of a lost experience that find their way back through a dream, rather than through memory images in wakefulness. These forgotten events use the avenue of a dream but are not so much symbolic disguised products as they are direct recollections, resembling a photograph. *Wielopole, Wielopole* has the characteristics of that process of return of memory segments in a dream.

The question is where exactly the objects of these forgotten memory units are being kept until they make their re-entry into the visible world, and why they are kept buried there. It would seem that these are precious objects, now lost, that cannot be given up and are, therefore, kept imprisoned, so to speak, in deep endopsychic crypts. Such psychic arrangements have been observed in clinical psychoanalysis during the process of mourning.[24] These crypts constitute, in effect, psychic *emballages*. Like Kantor's physical *emballages*, the loved objects are placed in secret cysts

> *when we want to shelter*
> *and protect,*
> *to preserve,*
> *to escape the passage of time.*
> *. . .*
> *when we want to*
> *hide something*
> *deeply.*
> $\qquad\qquad$ (*The Emballage*)[25]

The lost dead objects, "pathetic remains of greatness," are kept in the crypt, half-alive, half-dead, never allowed to die, in a vast psychic cemetery. This is particularly the case in *Wielopole, Wielopole*. As already mentioned, mourning under these conditions goes on forever.

These "*cadavres exquis*" are brought out of their hiding places/tombs to live their stories on the stage of memory, and each time they appear as actors in *different* scenaria. The *I*, in other words, is free to combine the elements of recollection *differently* each time. The scenes of memory constitute, therefore, a continuous "rehearsal" involving repeated de-constructions and re-constructions. Kantor, here, has understood intuitively what both the psychoanalyst and the neuroscientist have discovered. Memory of distant events is, essentially, a continuous process of retroactive construction. It "recalls" the past *of the present*, not the historical past which remains forever elusive. Images of isolated elements recalled – sometimes a single trait of a person or a specific situation – are repeatedly reshuffled (Kantor considers this a characteristic of childhood memories), thereby creating new sequences. In this endless repetition memory is in a constant state of flux, never stable:

> *Maybe this stubborn repetition of action,*
> *this pulsating rhythm*
> *which lasts as long as life;*
> *which ends in nothingness;*
> *which is futile;*
> *is an inherent part of MEMORY.*
> $\qquad\qquad$ (*The Room: Maybe a*
> $\qquad\qquad\qquad$ *New Phase*)[26]

Here we come to the central issue that obsesses Kantor regarding the mechanism of memory. Memory cannot re-capture its object. It not only fails to re-capture and re-instate the lost object, it – by its very nature – repeats and re-affirms the chasm between memory image and object. Our condition is, in fact, that of Plato's chained spectators in his Myth of the Cave who are constrained to view only the shadow of the object. Magritte's images remind us of the deception of the image: *Ceçi n'est pas une pipe*. Our wish to re-find the object is painfully frustrated as memory cannot seize it:

> *It is difficult to define*
> *the spatial dimensions of memory.*
> *THE ROOM is the one where I spent my childhood.*
> *A Dead Room*
> *inhabited by the Dead.*
> *I keep setting up*
> *the house, which is gone:*
> *it dies over and over*
> *together with the tenants*
> *who are my family.*
>   (*Wielopole, Wielopole, Director's Notes*)[27]

The entire production of *Wielopole, Wielopole* is replete with doubles, beginning with the title. A title that would express more explicitly the problematics of memory might be *(Wielopole), "Wielopole,"* where the bracketed name would indicate the inaccessibility of the original object, lost forever, while the quoted name would refer to its inauthentic *ersatz* reproduction. Kantor came to believe that Memory as Repetition is the ultimate Reality and the essence of Art, and made it, accordingly, the essence of his theater.[28] However, the "real structure of memory" is a "pulsating rhythm" of a ceaseless alternation of construction and destruction. Memory is, therefore, futile, a vain activity of grasping shadows that brings us face-to-face with Nothingness. Repetition cannot repeat the original. Moreover, the double in repetition turns out to be not the narcissistic double, but Girard's *double monstrueux*, the Great Other, Death. Like Freud's dream, considered to be the "royal road" to the "other world" of the Unconscious, repetition is the "royal road" to the "other world" of Death. Linear time, foreclosed in repetition, leads to the realm of eternity and nothingness. So the Real turns out in the end to be an illusion, and Art is, accordingly, a counterfeit. Repetition only demonstrates "the life-impotence of ILLUSION."[29] The memory image that appears to bring our lost object back is a deceptive, fraudulent impersonation, a masquerade of an object ineptly masking death. We are shamelessly betrayed, swindled by villains, defeated. The actors, those evil impersonators, are, thus, attacked and vilified by Kantor: they are "shady individuals . . . rumpled unwashed, sickly, deformed, basely made up to resemble" the loved lost object:

> *Let's admit it quite openly: the process of evoking memories*
> *is suspect and none too clean.*
> *It is simply a hiring agency.*
> *Memory makes use of "hired" characters.*
> *They are sinister individuals, mediocre and suspect creatures*
> *waiting to be "hired" like home-help by the hour.*
> *Almost crumbled, dirty, badly dressed, sickly,*
> *bastardized, acting out badly the parts of people*
> *often near and dear to us.*[30]

This sad arrangement brings out the tragic aspect of the failure of memory and the betrayal of art. *Wielopole, Wielopole* raises the question of the relation of Kantor's theater of memory to the tragic. Since Art is no more than a poor duplicate of the original, which remains radically and irrevocably separate from it and inaccessible, art is always a counterfeit. This, however, gives art "a measure of profundity and tragic fascination," which is accentuated and brought out poignantly by Kantor through the method of circus clownery, sarcasm and burlesque merged with the tragic. The tragic feeling arises from the gap that separates the *I* from its object imprinted in memory. This reflects the original rupture of the nascent *I* splitting off its matrix and leaving a fragment of its substance behind (the "primal loss") – a mythic event that we have considered to be an unconscious phantasy of the primal scene. Kantor's theater focuses specifically and intensely on this traumatic fracture that we posit as the foundation of all theater. The *I* is condemned to forever seek a re-union with its lost fragment (which is a selfobject) with the characteristic pathos and passion that Plato ascribes to the two split halves of *androgynon* "desperately yearning for each other" in order to reconstitute their original one-ness.[31] Plato points to the *limits* imposed on the self as the result of bisection. The scission opens up a gap and inaugurates the consequent conflict between the divine and the human (the main axis of Greek tragedy), but, also, between the mental (memory, fantasy) and the physical, or between illusion and reality (Kantor's preoccupation). The scission establishes the limits and limitations of human capacity. Kantor's doubles embody precisely that schism and express the tragic, as he admits to Bablet.[32] His twin actors are tragic characters, he explains, specifying that "the true actor is very sad inside, comical and tragic." The same dynamic of cleavage and limits obtains in the encounter between spectator and actor located "on the other side," or between Kantor on stage and his objects of memory. Human limitation demands a tragic submission to Necessity. Kantor's inevitable failure to a bridge over memory and its object, the present and the absent, the sacred and the garbage, the human and the divine brings his theater close to tragedy and makes Kantor – resolute in his stubborn stance *à la frontière* – a tragic hero.

In *Wielopole, Wielopole* there is no sign that the irreversibility of the rupture and the human failure to re-appropriate the lost object can be tolerated, or that the violence of death can be endured. Repetition allows a denial of loss while ontologic grief endlessly re-enters from the back door. The violence of the foundational schism soon breaks loose and creates havoc on stage in the scene of The Last Supper:

> *Leonardo's painting, which I have always deeply admired, arouses in me a sort of perverse urge to desecrate its superhuman order and calm, and to bring it down to earth by means of an act of violence.*
>
> (*Wielopole, Wielopole, Director's Notes*)[33]

The violence contained in The Last Supper, shortly before Christ's death, unfolds in parallel with the warm, gentle mood of birth evoked by the simultaneous Christmas carol played by the dead-alive Deportee. The central feature of The Last Supper is betrayal. The violence of the primal scene as a sort of betrayal of life by death explodes leading, here, to a frightful regression to an earlier state of chaos, un-integration, life–death interchangeability (the rotating death-bed) and the dominion of EroThanatos:

> *A stampede of EVACUEES*
> *FLIGHT,*
> *DISASTER,*
> *the cries of the FAMILY,*
> *a total breakdown,*
> *disintegration,*
> *exposure . . .*
>   (Wielopole, Wielopole,
>   *Director's Notes*)[34]

This is an orgy fueled by a seething magma of primitive sexual and death energy:

> *A HELL, A WHOREHOUSE*
> *THE LAST JUDGEMENT,*

THE APOCALYPSE

. . .

Auntie Manka reaches religious orgasm with the DUMMY Priest.
The DUMMY Helka is raped by the SOLDIERS,

. . .

orgasmic movements,
plenty of CROSSES,
as in a graveyard.

(Wielopole, Wielopole, *Director's Notes*)[35]

The wound is wide open again, as raw as ever, and the only desperate relief can come by resorting to its reproduction in Art (Theater):

Slowly in the general LEVELING DOWN of this hellish circus
a REPRODUCTION appears, a dim reflection
of the familiar picture of The Last Supper.
The soldiers perform rifle drill over the long table.
The civilians (the FAMILY) vainly imitate the gestures of the apostles.

In this way this (hopefully) LAST supper is celebrated,
while the CAROL makes it seem like Christmas Eve . . .
(*Wielopole, Wielopole, Director's Notes*)[36]

Before any question of a possible movement towards integration can be raised at this point, a subtle "protective" function of memory must be considered. The epistemology of memory resorts here to the meta-psychology of memory. It has been observed that certain childhood memories serve as a "screen" that both covers up and bears a reflection of earlier highly charged traumatic experiences from infancy.[37] Those earlier memories cannot be comprehended or recalled because they belong to a pre-verbal or even pre-mental stage, to Aulagnier's *originaire*. That was a bodily, pre-representational phase whose experiences are, in principle, unknowable because they cannot be made the object of thought and cannot be dreamed directly. They provide the material, however, for the formation of primal phantasies such as the primal scene. The question we wish to raise here is whether Kantor's frustrating, treasonous memory that is radically and irreversibly *severed* from its object "screens" and reflects the originary traumatic schism of the primal scene, presenting it in a second version, and, thereby, making it less noxious. That primal event remains inaccessible to dreams or thoughts, but returns here as a *forme fruste*, as the "obscure cataclysm" that killed the PLATOON conscripts, the betrayal in Leonardo's Last Supper that *indicate* the End of the World, Apocalypse. It may, also, return as the recollection of common, ordinary events or situations that assume cosmic proportions and are experienced as catastrophic. For example, a street corner:

> *From this corner my mother disappeared,*
> *when she went away for a long period,*
> *round that bend*
> *which was the **End of the World**.*
> (*Wielopole, Wielopole*)[38]

So, memory "betrays" and frustrates the reminiscing subject by not yielding its *real* object, yet, in re-enacting, as it were, what cannot be remembered, it also betrays its *object* in a subtle way while concealing it. But, in carrying out this complex procedure memory also functions as a shield (cf. Perseus' shield) against the unlivable original catastrophic event.

The epistemological *aporiae* of memory directly affect the question of identity. Identity requires a degree of integration and coherence that is rendered problematic by memory's "pulsating rhythm that ends in nothingness," by its unexpected discontinuities and its erratic track. The self in *Wielopole, Wielopole* is multiply fractured. Memory fails in its function to re-capture the past: the memory trace left by the lost object is *not* the real object, and this leads to existential doubts and a grievous crisis. The schismatic self appears as the *I*, but also as the Impersonator and as the lost, dead, un-retrievable *I*, a vital fragment of some lost paradisiacal one-ness that was left behind.

The *I* is left face-to-face with its dispersed mobile fragments on the other side of the mirror:

> *MYSELF:*
> *Sitting in the center of the stage. The text of my part, as follows,*
> *must remain unspoken.*
> *Here is my Grandmother*
> *. . .*
> *Now they are in the room, imprinted as memories*
> *. . .*
> *From this moment on, their "dates and fortunes" begin to change*
> *passing through a series of radical alterations . . .*[39]

Kantor and his family, the dreamer and his dream, occupy radically different spaces, on either side of a barrier and their encounter is shocking. Divided, disassociated, yet uncannily similar. Two *I*'s are confronted with each other,

> *confronted with our own image*
> *with which we must become REUNITED.*[40]

The doubling of identity leads to confusion and anguish accentuated by Kantor's ruthless mockery. The Priest is confused with the Dummy Priest, Uncle Olek with Uncle Karol. Who is who? Whom do we mourn, the Priest or the Dummy Priest? The Uncles devise a clever test to distinguish between the two Priests (the body cannot lie). The two identical identities are, despite everything, distinct. A deep gap separates them: the PLATOON here, the FAMILY opposite, the dead here, the living–dead there. Frames frozen in time. Superimposed. Confusion. The grieving family of the dead Priest on the rotating bed must take a position vis-à-vis an inescapable Either–Or that is embodied in and articulated by the infernal Machine of Death:

> *That's not him*
> *that's not the real one*
> *he's not one of us . . .*

The bed/Machine of Death turns round:

> *Oh, oh, oh look here he comes.*[41]

while the other half of the FAMILY leans on the opposite side of the identity dis-junction. The ineradicable ambiguity causes a pervasive absurdism that subverts meaning. Fractured identities garishly parade around led by mad Auntie Manka/You-know-Who/Himmler/Rabbi and her polymorphous language, Polish, Yiddish, Hunnish barking, or quoting from the Gospels in perfect articulation, while she is disconnected from her surroundings caught in the grip of apocalyptic religious frenzy and "counting the hours before the impending catastrophe." There is little that would point clearly to a movement of integration in this disordered world of turmoil, agitation and meaninglessness bordering on dementia. And so, Kantor's role on stage, somewhere between his dream and the spectator, becomes a little clearer now. Does he point to an "exit"?

> *I take* [the Priest] *by the hand and we slowly walk off together.*
> *Then I come back, fold up the tablecloth with infinite care,*
> *put it under my arm*
> *and exit.*
>
> (*Wielopole, Wielopole, Director's Notes*)[42]

Wielopole, Wielopole, nevertheless, does seem to move towards a new perspective of the existential fracture and a new approach in dealing with – "colluding with" – the foundational trauma. There is a suggestion of a changed relation of the dreamer to his dream. There are moments when the dreamer *à la frontière* enters his dream, intimating a movement towards integration. There are distinct photographic plates of memory belonging to different times and diverse contexts (historical, social, religious, personal) that are superimposed and, although they create absurd situations at times, they engage in a dynamic play of interaction that has the potential of moving toward integration. The separating barrier functions also as a *mirror* and this "positional arrangement" – shocking though it may be – points to a certain collusion between the two separate and distinct sides, a movement towards a unified bi-focal identity. This subtle process of the two sides sliding into each other is brought to a peak in the overlapping between the violence of the Last Supper–betrayal–death on the one hand and Christmas–birth on the other. Chopin composed the Scherzo in B minor as an exile in Vienna, while Poland, crushed, was once again in turmoil. In the midst of rage and agitation, faintly and slowly, from far away an old Christmas carol returns to him, the upheaval recedes, "Poland has not perished yet." A sparkle of hope – the developmental achievement of the depressive position – is the only guarantee that the nascent *I* can survive and grow after the psychic turmoil of the primal scene. We note that the old Polish carol finds its way into the scherzo, but it is not repeated there: it is transformed, as is the whole scene. The ancient psychic wound (the primal scene) is not to be merely repeated. This wouldn't suffice. It must be transformed, re-dreamed[43] – once again, a point of convergence of psychoanalysis and theater. Kantor never stops changing, repeating, destroying, restructuring, re-dreaming his dream: an endless "rehearsal." This is clear as he moves from one production to another, or within the course of a given production. In his *Director's Notebook* we read: "Looking afresh over the notes from the last rehearsal, I am disappointed," so he reformulates everything. Or, he comments "I still want to give free play to my imagination," as he is not satisfied after the last rehearsal. He emphasizes that it is this continuous spontaneous visions and revisions of the rehearsal that constitute the "writing" of the score.

Returning to the ending of *Wielopole, Wielopole*, the ritualistic folding of the tablecloth by Kantor himself generates an emotionally charged, multi-determined state in the spectator. This slow, serene gesture allows, perhaps, a vague allusion to a possible closure of the drama of helpless confusion and sadness, as if Kantor were saying to the spectator "*Ite Missa est,*" i.e., "Go, now, and repeat the Old Story: Betray me, remember me, lose me." The human destiny of the ontologically necessary tragic rupture and irretrievable loss will be repeated *ad infinitum*. But, perhaps, the grief will be better tolerated.

Death the Organizer

Once again, five years have passed since the second piece of the Theater of Death trilogy. In *Let the Artists Die*, the last play of the trilogy, Kantor, for the first time, appears as one of the *dramatis personae*. He is on stage, but it seems less as the conductor of a Dance of Death and more as a witness-participant, quietly and reflectively sitting on his half-broken chair on the side. *Let the Artists Die* is more openly self-referential with a focus on Kantor's *I*, or, rather, his *I*'s. Once again we are in the space of a dream. Although not a nightmare, this is certainly an anxiety dream. Kantor's "poor room of imagination" is flooded by the onrush of his multiple selves, various fragments of his *I*. Face-to-face with multiple memory spaces – fragments of experiences of past and future, of fantasy and unconscious phantasy – the *I* is called upon to construct articulating mobile, flexible and alterable links.

The central focus here is the ontological problem of identity that Kantor considers to be the chief concern of art:

> *He* [the character] *pursues a search of his own self.*
> *It seems to me that this strange symptom*
> *is a metaphor*
> *that refers to the deepest meaning of art and of life*
> . . .
> *I am engaged in a search for myself!*
> *Myself, I create another myself . . .*
> *Face-to-face!*
> *It's a kind of madness.*
> (Guide to the performance,
Let the Artists Die)[44]

In the comical pantomime of the twin characters of the AUTHOR and MYSELF DYING, in Act I, the *I* is shown to be where it is absent, and to be absent in its presence:

> *I am here, so I can leave*
> *Have I left?*
> . . .
> *I am gone.*
> *And yet I am here.*
> *I have gone mad.*

This disturbing situation of the *I* facing its own absence comes into sharper focus in the scene that ensues: the AUTHOR is now face-to-face with

MYSELF DYING. It is death that will, finally, bring an end to the confusion of identity: the MYSELF DYING is dead while the AUTHOR
is mourning his dead "twin." The dead is other, different and distinct. In
the self-portrait scene of Act II, however, the two become indistinguishable again, mirror images of each other and the *I* embraces both: that
dead person is *I-DEAD*. The tragic pathos of the situation of ontological
rupture and reunification with the split-off part is accentuated – as is characteristic of Kantor – by ingenious clowning. However, the *I-AUTHOR*
will not tolerate the merge for long and will suddenly jump out of the
death-bed where he had been lying with his double.

In *Let the Artists Die*, we see the various fragments of the *I* in action:
the *I*-REAL PERSON, "the main perpetrator of all this"; the AUTHOR
describing his own dying; the *I*-DYING; the *I*-AT THE AGE OF 6; and,
finally, the *I*-WIT STWOSZ who is also Kantor's alter ego here. Kantor
as a stage personage enters the action twice: first, when the Proprietor
of the cemetery addresses him directly while describing his woes and,
second, when Aesculapius takes Kantor's pulse, after being told that "*he*"
(Kantor on stage) is the same as the Author, the *I*-DYING and the *I*-AT
AGE 6. Thus, we have the *I* in multiple contexts of Now–Then, Here–
There, Dead–Living.

The "*I* in search of itself" will search for a degree of cohesiveness and
coherence that would give it a sense of "wholeness." This can only be
achieved through the establishment of a *relation* with its various objects,
i.e., the objects in its multifarious experiential situations. And this is only
possible if there is acceptance of the different, the "Other," and, ultimately, if there is toleration of the revolutions of time and of loss. The
establishment of a relation is a process of "construction." A relation is
the result of what is, fundamentally, a *creative* process. Art finds its roots
here. In *Let the Artists Die*, the *I* is "thrown" (in the Heideggerian sense of
Geworfen) into the INFERNUM of the Room, the Infernum of ordinary
life, which is crowded with the dead parts of the self, the wreckage of history, the cheap comedy of life. The Room, the prison cell of the artist, is
in constant mutation: a cemetery, a shelter for the outcasts, the battlefield
of history, a prison, an artist's studio, a barricade. And here it must create.
Kantor was significantly influenced in this production by Malczewski's
vision of the artist and his work, particularly by the manner that this is
allegorically depicted in two of Malczewski's masterpieces, *Vicious Circle*
and *Melancholia*. The artist's *I*, the artist's identity, is shown here as it
relates to history and to the whirlpool of time. Time, in its destabilizing
effects, is the only organizing principle. From our perspective, the *I* seeks
to heal its inherent wound (the primal fragmentation) through the "construction" of a transforming *relation with its objects*, a relation that tolerates
the undulations of time.

Time in *Let the Artists Die* is time collapsed so that the past and the future exist as an actuality in the present – the actual of theater. The past self (child) and the future self (dying) achieve an organic interstitial relationship so the experience of dying could now apply to the past, as well as to its repetition in the future self.

> *We advance towards the future*
> *as we, at the same time, delve deeper*
> *into the regions of the past, into the regions of death.*[45]

The rupture of being (Winnicott's "breakdown"[46]) that had *already* taken place at the moment of mythic origin (primal scene) but had remained un-represented until now – a "bizarre" element (Bion[47]) that could not become the object of thought – could now attain a degree of "figurability,"[48] be "contained" by the artist's self and be re-lived in the present as its future repetition. The projection of the *I* to its future "part," or rather, the introjection of the future into the actual *I*, brings death to the core of the *I*. This nucleus of death can now provide structure to the *I*. Kantor's attention was drawn to the unifying power of death when he came across the work of Unilowski:

> *I discovered a similar process in the work of Zbigniew Unilowski, titled A Shared Room where from the first to the last pages, we are witnesses of the DEATH of the hero of the novel. Even more unusual is the fact that the author, in this work, describes . . . his own death.*
> 　　　　　　　　　　　　　　(*Let the Artists Die, Program Notes*)[49]

And Kantor specifies:

> *In this piece* [Let the Artists Die] *I want death to gather together the various symptoms of life; I want death to become almost the structure of the piece.*

He achieves this by a rich superimposition of photographic negatives – a process that is given here greater accent than in *Wielopole, Wielopole* – of plates linked together, bonded by the common thread of death. Thus, the various fragments of the self from birth to death seem to come together here, joined through the centripetal force of death that ties them from within. Death provides the glue that will allow and sustain a relation of the different *I*'s with their objects and with each other. This is the creative potential of Death and the foundation of art according to Kantor. The simultaneous presence of the images of the various plates that overlap in a sort of transparent palimpsest abolishes a mutually excluding "Either–Or," replacing it with an integrating "This *and* That."

Splitting as an existential condition now yields its place to an inescapable *ambivalence* that is the price of unification of the self.

Death at the core of the *I*, however, operates a dis-junction between the *I-living* and its "spit image" (*Self-Portrait* in Act II), the *I-dead*. Death the Organizer is, also, Death the divider. The two fragments of the *I* – identical yet different – are brought together through a mirror that joins them, which, however, also constitutes an ambiguous barrier that separates them. Here, the *I-living* sees its reflection as *I-dead*:

> *Two superimposed images, one belonging to the reality of our experience while the other seems to be coming from "beyond."*[50]

Kantor specifies:

> *I want to restore to the word reflection its essential meaning and implications which are tragic . . .*
>
> (*Reflection*)[51]

The tragic is precisely the result of a cleavage instituted by the barrier. The part of the *I* and its reality that is on the "other side" of the mirror is "put behind bars," incarcerated in a prison, buried in a grave, says Kantor, which is another way of speaking about what the psychoanalyst calls "repression" to the Unconscious. The principal task of Kantor's theater is a determination to unearth that "other side" and link it with this side of our experiential daily reality. He speaks of this project as an *extension* of our reality towards the "other side" and its own specific laws.[52] This expansion of the living *I* to the "other side" is audacious and has a heavy emotional cost. Kantor's theater, as he frequently reminds us, is a theater of emotions. Yet, despite the cost, Kantor believes there is something vital to be gained by this process of psychic expansion to the regions of the dead and the repressed *I*, i.e., the part of the *I* that lies buried in the Unconscious.

Death's vehicle being Time, Kantor's Theater of Death echoes Heidegger's basic thoughts on this matter.[53] Heidegger, too, was concerned with a well-rounded, authentic existence that integrates Time and Death to become a "whole" Dasein. Klein's "whole" object is another version of the same idea. Both, a whole Dasein and a whole object require a recognition and acceptance of Death and of loss (non-being, absence). Death, in Heidegger, belongs to the "Being" of the Dasein. As in Kantor, the individual's being can move towards itself only by advancing towards the future while moving towards its past simultaneously. The authentic Dasein effectuates a leap forward in time, "getting ahead of itself" (*Vorlaufen*), rendering through this act the potentiality of death actual. This is the Dasein's position of "Being-towards-Death" which describes well Kantor's conception of the Real, as well as the task of theater in constructing an extended, integrated identity across barriers and gaps. Significantly, in Heidegger, as in Kantor, Death and temporality are what structure human reality (Dasein) and the *I*.

Malczewski's *Vicious Circle* re-appears in *Let the Artists Die* as the whirlpool of the dead and their crosses, of generals and soldiers, saltimbanques, corpses, pimps, prostitutes and prisoners, the whole chorus led by the artist-little-boy-Kantor[54] who, as *I-REAL* at the age of 64 at the other end of the circle, closes the sad parade of victory and defeat: TEATRUM MORTIS ET GLORIAE. What provides, paradoxically, the bridge that closes the Circle is the "vicious" irreversibility of linear time. Thus, a continuity is established – an "extension" – that unites the vibrant, vivacious bright side of the Circle with the dark side on the other side. Victory parade and funeral procession are inextricably joined forever. This curious, paradoxical conjunction is tolerated and fueled by the forces of life: Eros. Time and Thanatos (the radical rupture) are, nonetheless, acknowledged, brought in by Aesculapius, "Doctor of Greek origins" who, measuring the beat of the pulse, can announce death only in Greek:

Τεθνήξει μετ' ολιγας ωρας.

In the Guide to the performance, Kantor explains that:

> *The visit of the doctor allows the concealment behind the clownish laughter and black humor of a true tragedy.*

Behind the clowning, there is, also, an unmistakable atmosphere of mourning – perhaps most poignant in the song of the "You-Know-Who" riding his skeleton-horse.

The Artist-Death remains steadfast at the border in Malczewski's *Melancholia* and is accurately reproduced on Kantor's stage with Mother as the immobile dark figure downstage between the Inferno and the spectators, while the Artist-Kantor sits on his chair stage left. In his Studio-Prison Cell, Kantor-Wit Stwosz-Death in his black cape and hat creates a monument of the tortured characters of the human Comedy. The artist's residence is the "other side" of the barrier, located in the chambers of Death. An outcast, a menace to "reality" (illusion), he must be sequestrated for the safety of the public – exactly as Freud had thought with reference to the Unconscious and the primitive forces residing therein.

Kantor formulates a "meta-psychology of prison" (he calls it "ontology-eschatology"). For the artist, this dungeon holding chaotic forces of life and death is his natural habitation. And his mission is to revolt, to break out of the prison (the "return of the repressed"), to free the locked up creative primitive energies, to spread his message to the world and to build barricades against illusion. If identity is to be authentic, it must incorporate *both sides* of the divided self. This was Kantor's unfaltering mission in the various and diverse forms that his art and life took. The Artist, in Kantor's view the spokesman of Time and Death, is called upon to give structure to the tragic fragmentation of human reality. It is Art and, more specifically, Theater that aims to be the final Unifier, the force that strives to gather together the dispersed and disparate fragments of identity and fashion them into a cohesive whole that is conscious and tolerant of its inner contradictions. Through the bringing together of opposite psychic regions and fostering a communication between them art generates meaning:

> *I feel . . . that they* [the chance elements] *have a shared cause and I get the vague impression that are guided by some hand . . .*
> *(Let the Artists Die, Program Notes)*[55]

Meaning emerges out of a relation, out of a "shared cause."

The "therapeutic" aspect of theater did not escape Kantor. The extension of the self across the barrier towards the "other side" to join up[56] with its other half is most important and beneficial, he says:

> *Something far more important is: The extension of our reality beyond its boundaries so that we can better cope with it in our lives.*
> *(Reflection)*[57]

Zaduszki

In *I Shall Never Return*, we have a very different type of "personal confession." Kantor is not merely telling us – or telling himself – about himself; he is *showing* himself to us by assembling all of his part-selves together in a sort of personal *zaduszki*.[58] This shift of perspective presupposes and entails several significant changes in the *I* of the actor-Kantor, in the *I* of the spectator, in the *I* of the subject. A "confession" – in the dynamics of the psyche – implies a scrutinizing eye of a Judge. In this "Last Judgment" Kantor is both the judged and the Judge. He is the actor and the conscience of the century, and so is the spectator. In the unrelenting exposition of his phantasies and his nightmares, Kantor lays bare his vulnerabilities, insecurities, fears, doubts, cruelties and hopes. And his guilt. An element of quiet sadness and mourning permeates the space from beginning to end. It carries with it the realization that scars cannot be reversed, cannot be undone, that losses are irreversible, that defeat must be acknowledged and evil "endured."[59] This evil is a sort of meta-physical evil beyond human control, about which, however, humans *must* feel guilty to be able to live with each other. This conundrum can only be confronted if one occupies a position "on the verge of time" in this shabby Inn of solitude, of pure existence, of poor existence, where "things lose their ordinary meaning"[60] when one "falls asleep and wakes up inside, staring at the ceiling with blind eyes."

The artist's struggle towards integration of the various fragments of the self and their relations is much more advanced in *I Shall Never Return*. This is because here, more than in *Let the Artists Die*, Kantor is on stage as an active persona; in fact, he is the protagonist:

> *I always stood at the door and waited. And now I am sitting in the middle, an important person.*[61]

"He always wanted to be in the center!" the English Lady/part-of-his-*I* will maliciously comment. Kantor's "creations" are certainly not very friendly towards him. Fragmentation makes inner conflict and opposition inescapable. And this explains the wish to "defenestrate" (project) the accusing parts of the self, to split them off and leave them behind for good, as Kantor threatens to do here. But they will follow him "like a shadow," say the Hasidim. *This* is what needs to be endured. And, in this production, it is.

The haphazard superimposition of photographic negatives is even more complex and bewildering here, as compared to *Let the Artists Die*. The Inn/Shelter/Classroom/Church/Concentration camp will host all the characters from Kantor's previous productions who will, however, play each other's roles, assigned to them by some invisible force at random. Characters, roles and acts are all mingled and freely interchangeable. Thus, for example, the twin Hasidim from *The Water Hen* dance the Cardinals' tango from *The Snows of Yesteryear*, the Woman with a Rat-Trap from *Dainty Shapes and Hairy Apes* becomes Telemachus in the Odysseus scene, the Innkeeper is transformed into Odysseus, and they all become the poor wrecks on the school benches of *The Dead Class*.

As Kantor joins up with all his selves, phantasies, fantasies and memories, his real physical self and his mental creations, his inside world and the outside of his art productions, his life, phantasy and art, all of these come together coalescing into a whole that is rather of the nature of a multi-colored mosaic. A convergence to this degree had not been attempted

before. This amalgam creates its own space: the space of the *I*. It is a unified space with porous or fluid boundaries that allows a constant exchange
between "inside" and "outside." Kantor is no longer focused here on the
space of the "other side," troubled and energized by the duality of radical
difference, but is constructing, instead, a unified space of existence, the
space inhabited by the *whole I*. It is a space with constantly shifting borders, always in a process of demolition and reconstruction. How else can
Eros dialogue with Thanatos? The *I* is a "work-in-progress." Phantasy
and reality, the present and the absent, Love and Death ("the moment
came when I could not tell the one from the other"), the *I* and the Other
meet in a spatial continuum that encompasses both sides.

But, as expected, the joining force of the fragments, the thread that
ties them together in this their Last Dance, is Death.

The performance opens with the familiar persistent tormenting rattle
of the crib-coffin. The couple of Kantor and his Bride are married and
buried behind the door while the church organ plays what sounds like
a funeral tune. The eerie band of the Nazi Violinists advance while the
poor terrified Rabbi runs for his life. The wailing *Ani maanim* of the
Dishwasher is heard again and again – marching to the gas chambers. The
murdered Marian Kantor fastened to his torture machine-Cross ("*Morts*")
is brought in while we hear his distant voice "I died on the 24th of
January 1944" and the camp loudspeaker announcing emphatically his
death of a heart attack. The Ironclad Violinists dress up the Innkeeper
as Odysseus who will soon follow the crowd of the shades. Kantor reads
from his 1944 notes: "In my own homeland I walked into a graveyard."
Charon's bathtub-boat appears out of nowhere, followed by the throng
of ghosts. The Inn is now Auschwitz and Katyn, the mass grave-Holo-
caust, Last Emballage of the century. And, finally, in person, the Black
Lady Herself "who rules the entire performance." A Dance of Death. As
Kantor insisted, it is Death that provides structure, coherence and meaning to human existence.

The coming together of the different segments of the self cannot occur
until the painful psychic process of mourning takes place. It is the work
of Kadmus the Mourner to assemble together the scattered pieces of the
"mourned" Pentheus and restore Agave's shattered mind. The mourning
mood is not new, but, here, it heavily permeates the whole atmosphere. It
is, perhaps, best expressed by the sorrowful recurring Chopin Scherzo of
Uncle Stasio-Phemius. The part he is playing is not the scherzo part, but
the section in the middle, designated by Chopin as "Molto Più Lento."
And, in any event, isn't Kantor at the threshold – the threshold of a grave –
in a permanent state of mourning? *Molto importante!*, he stresses, at the
door of the tomb that is also a womb (*Lulajze Jesuniu*[62]).

Odysseus shows him what to read from his old notes:

> *In my own homeland I uncovered hell. I walked into a graveyard . . . There is nothing ahead . . . The coast of Ithaka . . . Seagulls . . . No-one can return to the land of their youth. I had my homeland in my heart. Now it is in my desires. A shadow. I yearn for a shadow.*[63]

There is the mournful Wedding, the melancholy look on the Bride's face, but there is also the mourning for the Century of Catastrophe. The emotion is inexpressible, and this is poignantly underlined by the Innkeeper's standard vacuous comment "What a depressing story!" Yet he solemnly leads the Bride out with great gentleness as a sad organ tune is being heard. The wrenching doleful, but also angry and protesting, *Ani maanim* sung by the "slovenly" Dishwasher imposes a grave mood on the entire production. What is really the mourning for, if not for the necessary Evil, the Evil that renders the self "necessarily unhoused in being"? For an ancient stain traceable back to our origins? For a primal loss? Yet, it must be "endured" since it cannot be undone. However, if it is acknowledged it can be mitigated, it can become more tolerable and permit living – even more: creative living (Winnicott). What needs to be acknowledged – the central message of Greek tragedy never lost its relevance – is the necessary *limits* and limitations of human existence. Limits mean *loss*, irreversible loss of a perfect state, of "Paradise." Humans construct ideals in order to define their limitations. Ideals can be considered dysfunctional "side effects" of the overgrown human brain that has evolved in disharmony with the body: all dreams are nightmares.

In *I Shall Never Return*, Kantor shows us the long course of his journey, a journey he followed to its very end. He arrived at the point of not just recognizing, but perhaps coming to terms with his defeat: "No-one can ever return to the lost Paradise. I shall never return." There are many ways this can be heard, but among the meanings of this affirmation the central one would seem to be an authentic final admission that a return to an original fusional One-ness, to a state of completeness, is impossible. The loss created by the fracture of being, the foundational *manque à être* that resulted, cannot be reversed. It is mourning for the loss that will make the toleration of its finality possible. And it is mourning that will, then, allow the formation of a link with the lost object, a psychic link with the shadow of the object, a link fashioned by death. Such links connecting the subject with its lost objects (selfobjects) lead to the formation of a "whole subject," an object that has concatenated its dual nature of Eros and Thanatos.

A cohesive identity is a condition for the creation of meaning, insofar as meaning is the product of an object relation (which is always a shadow of the relation to the primary object, i.e., mother). Meaning will emerge from the re-staging of the primal trauma and the field of primary object relations associated with it. From the perspective adopted here, the "Trauma of the Century" is a "screen," in the psychoanalytic sense, for the original wound of the primal scene. In Kantor's theater, this original trauma is re-enacted in the Odysseus story. Odysseus returns from Stalingrad/Troy

> *to Cracow,*
> *to his Ithaka.*
> *Odysseus*
> . . .
> *who set the direction of my JOURNEY,*
> *after many years*
> *returns to my Dream*
> *of the Wedding . . .*[64]

"Troy" is Atlantis, "That night" of disaster, the End of the World. It is an echo of the birth–death event of the primal scene stored in unconscious phantasy. Half-dead, half-alive Odysseus, mutilated, re-appears on the stage. A murderer and a victim simultaneously.

> *I-Odysseus*
> . . .
> *I enter with HER.*
> *The BRIDE.*
> *Mine.*
> *Dead.*[65]

Kantor with his Bride/Helka/Penelope remain on the stage of *I Shall Never Return* to the end. Dead, or rather, half-dead. Helka with her torn veil, preserved forever, a precious emballage, kept dead-alive in a psychic crypt. A strong vitalizing bond that both defies and tolerates death. She, too, will never return – such are the ambiguities of human relations. But now meaning can be constructed out of this forever enigmatic relationship between Love and Death. Meaning and hope. The "un-burial" of the "Pompeii of the Century" by the Great Χρονος liberates the corpses who are then free to walk through the Door to the dark spaces behind, to their final grave. Is this an indication of hope that the dead can be finally allowed to die and become the objects of memory? In other words, be forgotten?

Ladies and Gentlemen, you will watch me.
And afterwards you can forget me . . .[66]

This forgetting, i.e., allowing the dead to exist only as objects of memory, liberates those who remain – the "remnants" – to live and to dream new dreams.

And so,

All, as usual in the end,
leave the stage.
I am left alone.
With my BRIDE.
It is HER who closes the performance.
I am only to help her.
"Après vous"
and:
I shall never return[67]

Kantor never returned. His *Birthday*, about three years later, was on the day of his death, a final confirmation that his life was his art.

Crossing over

Today Is My Birthday is a production that is dramatically different from anything that preceded it. It is unique in a very special way. Kantor is a visual artist, a painter who theatricalizes his paintings. However, here he goes beyond that. This "going beyond" is precisely the core theatrical event in this production and is what makes it singular among his works. Let us remind ourselves that *Today Is My Birthday* is a *rehearsal* and that what we see is the repetition of a rehearsal that will always repeat itself.

Kantor decides to move his living quarters on stage:

engulfed within this gnawing turbulence of
reflections, feelings, doubts and hopes,
I need to set my past in order
. . . .
My room on stage . . .
A real action. Let us assume so.
I have decided to move in and live onstage –
I have here my bed, my table, my chair, and, of course, my paintings.
I have often imagined my room in a theater,

> *inside of the theater,*
> *onstage, rather than in a hotel.*
>
> (*My Room*)[68]

We may suspect that the reason for this move is that he plans to show us *another side* of himself, a side we have not seen until now. We are intrigued by the "room inside the theater," a theatrical (real) space within the space of theater, which presents us with three frames of reality, one inside the other. What trick is he preparing for us this time?

Let us imagine that we are watching the rehearsal of December 7, 1990, in the auditorium of Grunwaldzka street. Kantor is walking around, agile, pensive, correcting movements, the position of objects, etc. The rehearsal proceeds as usual, but perhaps with a sense of urgency: "engulfed within this gnawing turbulence of reflections, feelings . . . I need to set my past in order . . . for my next production." This looks like the usual struggle of the artist to constitute himself or to unravel himself. This time he *constructs* reality:

> *Onstage (sic!),*
> *I am putting together (CONSTRUCTING)*
> *my POOR room of imagination.*
>
> (*A Painting*)[69]

His aim is, as usual, to orchestrate a clash between fiction and reality and to destroy Illusion. His technique, here, is one of visual double negatives:

> *The existence of the PAINTING and its interior*
> *in this production create the illusion of the SECOND DEGREE,*
> *in the presence of which my Poor Room*
> *onstage*
> *(which could be seen as illusion)*
> *becomes reality.*
>
> (*A Painting*)[70]

But what is specific to this production – and this is underlined by Kantor – is that here *a threshold is crossed.* We had seen this in his series of paintings under the title *Further on, Nothing*, where figures would extend outside the frame, their parts becoming three-dimensional. In *Today Is My Birthday*, the Self-Portrait, for example, will fall out of the frame and will cross over into reality. What is achieved through this move is a continuity between the "inside" and the "outside" of the *I*, between phantasy/fantasy and reality, between this side and the "other side" of the mirror.

This continuity bridges over the parts of the *I* that had been split and introduces ambivalence to the psyche. Kantor, like the Freudian *Ich*, occupies a place at the border between the two sides, looking alternatively to his front and to his back, keeping a tense, balanced position of equidistance between the two. The *I* is, thus, constituted as a "whole." But not for long. The "Organs of Power" burst into the Room and transform it into a battlefield. Troy. Everything is demolished. There is chaos, fragmentation, disintegration. All structure is undone: the *I* at the mercy of History, at the mercy of its own internal forces of annihilation. "History" destroys our most precious ideals, our *cadavres exquis* – emballages that we had hidden in our secret crypts. The *I* is, once more, confronted with the "Other," caught in a duel with the "Other," assailed by a fierce onslaught of the "Other": the Other as History, the "Other" as the Unconscious, the "Other" as Thanatos. The "Other," also, as Logos: the *I*, born into language, is necessarily submitted to the originary violence that shaped it into a "speaking *I*" that incorporated the violence intrinsic to Logos. We witness here the sudden destabilization of the *I*, its mutilation, its short journey from construction to dissolution, its *tragic* "defeat" – Aeschylus waving to us from the distance.

It is the Poor Girl who holds the only hope: sadness is the only escape from madness. She speaks in a foreign language: *c'est tellement triste*. She takes us from paranoid madness to depressive sadness, to another language. There is pain, but there is, also, compassion and even toleration in her attitude, in her body.

The victims will now make their appearance. Jaremianka stages a revolt against soft human tissue, impure, weak and emotional, destined to immobility in the grave. She will maintain unending Motion in Abstraction.[71] This is *her* shelter. It, strangely, meets up, thus forming a continuum, with its opposite at the other end: emotion, the "magnificent History of the individual human life" (*To Save from Oblivion*),[72] which is Kantor's shelter in his Poor Little Room. We need shelters. Stern's shelter was a grave (but, ah, that fly, life's ruthless self-mockery in the grave!). And now, we begin to suspect what trick Kantor was secretly planning on us. He had already told us: theater is a shock, an unexpected meeting with the Other from the "other side," the Absent One.

We are now, about a month later, spectators in the rehearsal of *Today Is My Birthday* in Toulouse, on the 10th of January, 1991. We look again. The chair, stage left, is empty. "A *real* action." He *had* warned us.

A few years earlier, the idea of a "leap" had been taking shape in his mind:

*In this theater of a formidable
and ruthless war,*

I make
(onstage)
the most risky and desperate maneuver
of my life.

I am almost certain
that it should ensure
victory.
I believe it will be so,
though I know that this victory cannot happen here,
here in this world,
I SHALL BE A VICTIM.
                              (*To Save from Oblivion*)[73]

So the time had come for his "supreme theatrical act." His *Birthday* was to be his *Deathday*, an uncanny confirmation of a primordial identity twin-ship imprinted on the phantasy of the primal scene: "Birth was the death of him."[74]

Theater – Kantor's Theater more specifically – enacts the unconscious phantasy of the original rupture-death. It repeats in the here-and-now the fractures of History, which themselves repeat an original break. Theater repeats the repetitions of the original trauma in the dark Chambers of the Polish King, *La vida es sueño.*[75]

The Self-Portrait falls out of his frame, Kantor falls out of his stage frame, the threshold is crossed. Illusion is defenestrated and "a *real* action" finally takes place. As Odysseus returned to a Room *really* destroyed by war in 1944, so Kantor *really* falls out of his stage frame into the reality of Death in 1990. *Q.E.D.* "Intensified realism." Is this Kantor's "victory"? In this "act," his presence and absence are linked, forming a continuum, the *I-living*, and the *I-dead* truly integrated into a "whole": a paradoxical *tous egaux* pronounced by Doctor Klein (a relation to Melanie Klein?). Herakleitos this time, waving from a distance:

> *The same thing exists in us living and dead, awake and sleep . . . because these having fallen into those, are those; and those, again, having fallen into these are these.*[76]

Kantor's funeral on the "Plank of Last Resort" at the end of the production slides off and "falls" into his real death.

Theater fosters the construction of a "whole *I*" by materializing the phantasy of the primal scene, i.e., by giving it body – a body whose absence creates a void – and investing it with meaning (Aulagnier' *mise-en-scène* leading to a *mise-en-sens*). Since the primal scene is "That night" when Death entered Life, Theater by enacting the primal scene "realizes" Death and places it at the center. This is what structures the *I*, and Kantor constructed his Theater of the Real – his Room – around that nucleus. Death, in his eyes, is the Final Organizer. We see in this Death's erotic aspect. In Kantor's last Morse message coming to us through *Today Is My Birthday* ("*Memoirs from Beyond the Grave*"[77]) the weight, the gravity of Reality, reaches an absolute level of intensity. Kantor achieves this by the method of double negatives, frames within frames, a "second degree illusion" that acts to undo itself. Here, without his mediation, it is *we* who are "at the border," this time alone. Ghosts of the Departed come directly to us. We unexpectedly find ourselves to be illegal intruders to the Room of Absence. Our position at the threshold

> *is not easy.*
> *The price one pays for it is*
> *a MEETING WITH DEATH.*
>   *(A Classroom)*[78]

And that was Kantor's plot from the beginning. The immediacy of Death seen from inside is most unsettling since, through the maneuver of the double negatives, we are confronted with *negative* apparitions, apparitions that do not appear. We have lost our shadows. The countenance of Death as the Final Organizer soon morphs into Thanatos, the Final Disorganizer. This is Freud's Thanatos who breaks links, dismembers unities and seeks a return to the Ur-Matter[79]: unquestionably, Death the monstrous "Organ of Power." Haydn's String Quartet is heard again, chaos, disarray, rampant disorder.

Death – we now understand – structures the *I* as a continuous process of construction, dismantlement, and reconstruction. This is the "pulse" of existence that Kantor speaks about. The *I* is permanently in a state of impermanence, in a dynamic state of constitution and destitution. Never stable, always in a process of becoming, always inclined towards being, it *gravitates* towards being. Theater as a framed activity reflects the process of the undulating oscillations and transformations of being. "All the world's a stage." Kantor's Theater of Death presents to us the metapsychology of Theater as the privileged locus of the *I*'s journey. With *Today Is My Birthday* Kantor's theater project – Theater's project – by an uncanny sleight-of-hand finally attains its elusive end.

The question of hope must be left last. Is there a space for hope in the Theater of Death? Kantor's Judaeo-Christian worldview would prompt him to lean towards that direction. The Last Supper of the Betrayal of Man is to be followed by His Return. But the tragic in Kantor has deep roots and leaves no room for soothing compromises, be they Euripidean or Christian. We may play the game "Collusions with the Plenum," but we know it's a game. The tragic hero constitutes himself in his defeat. Tragic trilogies – we must not forget – were followed by a satyr play that mocked man's Fatal impasses. Kantor's Circus is tragic. The "Eroica" reminds us of hopes deceived and brings in the tragic burlesque.

Yet, the Self-Portrait is running about in that final chaos holding the lamp close to his body. The flame *mustn't* be extinguished. Kantor can never completely explain his habit of returning on stage again and again, even though he knows that he can never really return. Is this man's hubris, his "tragic flaw," his rebellion against the gods, against Necessity? Rising up fully cognizant of his pre-destined defeat? The tragic hero's fall as an affirmation of his hope?

The space for hope is opened up by Kantor precisely in and around this destitute universe of "garbage" where he finds eternity, in this poor reality of the lowest rank. Here are the scars, the wounds of humanity, the stains that mark the *individual*. Hope exists only in recognition of the irreversibility of loss, in the wavering acceptance of indelible scars left following the attacks of destructive forces that inhabit the individual, and in the belief in the capacity for repair. The human impulse to perform acts of reparation has the characteristics of an *instinct*. It is what guarantees continued existence. However, the drive to repair is maintained only by the recognition and acceptance that the damage cannot be undone, that there is no return to the *status quo ante*, that the attempt to repair will leave a permanent scar that will always remind us of the original catastrophe. However, the potentiality of a human act remains as an answer to blind Necessity. It is only that feeble flickering flame behind the darkened cracked glass of the old battered lamp that will maintain the fissured cohesiveness of the *I* and allow life to continue.

Notes

1 Kobialka (2009), 393.
2 "From Hades [man] has found no escape" (Sophokles' *Antigone*, l. 360).
3 K. Pleśniarowicz, *The Dead Memory Machine*, trans. W. Brand (Aberystwyth: Black Mountain Press, 2004), 89.
4 *Ibid.*, 87.
5 That's what Kantor calls his characteristic mockery, sarcasm, irony – the burlesque.
6 T. Kantor, *The Dead Class*, *Director's Notebook* (Kraków: Cricoteka Archives, 1975).
7 Schulz (1974).
8 Program, *The Dead Class*, Première, November 15, 1975.
9 Ibid.

10 Ibid.
11 H. Segal, "Notes on symbol formation," *Int. J. Psycho-Anal.*, 1957: 135–141.
12 Freud, *S.E.* 12: 150.
13 Kobialka (2009), 404.
14 *Ibid.*, 414.
15 P. Brook, *The Empty Space* (New York: Touchstone, 1996), 121.
16 Freud, *S.E.* 18: 7–64.
17 Kobialka (2009), 384.
18 T. Kantor, *Entretiens* (Paris: Editions Carré, 1996), 57–58.
19 Kobialka (2009), 397.
20 *Ibid.*, 393.
21 Halczak (1991), 182.
22 Freud, *S.E.* 3: 301–323.
23 Freud, *S.E.* 2: 22.
24 See N. Abraham and M. Torok, *L'écorce et le noyau* (Paris: Flammarion, 1987).
25 Kobialka (2009), 158.
26 *Ibid.*, 368–369.
27 T. Kantor, *Wielopole, Wielopole,* trans. M. Tchorek and G.M. Hyde (London: Marion Boyars Publishers, 1990), 113.
28 *Ibid.*, 127.
29 *Ibid.*, 127.
30 Program, *Wielopole, Wielopole* (Kraków: Drukarnia Narodowa, 1984).
31 Plato (1973), *Symposium*, 191a and 193a: "For there was a time, I repeat, when we were one."
32 See D. Bablet, *Le théâtre de Tadeusz Kantor*, DVD vidéo (CNRS, 2006).
33 Kantor (1990), 134.
34 *Ibid.*, 135.
35 *Ibid.*, 136.
36 *Ibid.*, 136.
37 Freud *S.E.* 6:47.
38 Program, Wielopole, Wielopole (1984).
39 Kantor (1990), 17.
40 *Wielopole, Wielopole, Partytura*, in M. Kobialka (2009), 291.
41 Kantor (1990), 81.
42 *Ibid.*, 138.
43 A. Farro, "Transformations in dreams and characters in the psychoanalytic field," *Int. J. Psycho-Anal.*, 2009: 209–230.
44 Guide du spectacle *Qu'ils crèvent, les artistes*, translated by the author.
45 Ibid.
46 Winnicott (1974), 103–107.
47 Bion (1984), 36.
48 Botella (2013), 104–108. According to the Botellas' concept, figurability results from a process of dream-like regredience that recasts hitherto unrepresented psychic states into sensory images and then creates links between the various elements thereby producing meaning.
49 Avignon 1985 production Program Notes, translated by the author.
50 Guide du spectacle *Qu'ils crèvent les artistes*. Translated by the author.
51 Kobialka, (2009), 386.
52 cf. Rimbaud's *Je est un autre*. See A. Rimbaud, "Lettres du voyant," in *Oeuvres completes* (Paris: Pléiade, 2009), 339.

53 See Heidegger (1962).
54 This brings to mind Herakleitos' fragment claiming that Time is a boy playing draughts and that *his* is the Kingdom.
55 Pleśniarowicz (2004), 256.
56 It should be stressed that the bringing together of the two fragments of the *I* (the *I* and the *Other*) is not a re-union or fusion that reconstitutes the original One, but rather a *relation* in which each part recognizes itself in the other as being the same and yet different and separate.
57 Kobialka (2009), 386.
58 Polish All Souls Day commemorating the dead. The spirits of the dead are believed to return to their former homes on that day (November 2). The custom has ancient pagan roots.
59 Kobialka (2009), 319.
60 Halczak (1991), 172.
61 Kobialka (2009), 318.
62 Popular Polish Christmas carol.
63 See Kobialka (2009), 322.
64 Halczak (1991), 174.
65 *Ibid.*, 175.
66 Przewodnik, *Nigdy tu już nie powrócę*. See Kobialka (2009), 318.
67 Halczak (1991), 175.
68 Kobialka (2009), 488.
69 *Ibid.*, 494.
70 *Ibid.*, 496.
71 Program, Aujourd' hui c'est mon anniversaire, New York 1991: Letter to Maria Jarema.
72 Kobialka (2009), 390.
73 *Ibid.*, 391–392.
74 S. Beckett, *A Piece of Monologue*, in *Three Occasional Pieces* (London: Faber & Faber, 1982).
75 P. Calderon, *Life is a dream* (Mineola, NY: Dover Publications, 2002).
76 Kirk and Raven (1971), 189. Fragment 205. Translated by the author.
77 F.R. Chateaubriand, *Mémoires d' outre-tombe* (Paris: Le livre de Poche, 2001).
78 Kobialka (2009), 229.
79 Freud, *S.E.* 23: 148.

Epilogue

Adherence to and a comforting belief in "grand narratives" is long a thing of the past. The post-modern subject is irreversibly de-centered and condemned to a random and rapidly shifting locus of relativity. Multiple factors in interaction have played a role in this development. Technological advances that have acquired their own momentum beyond human mastery, wars and wars of ideology, the exploration of heretofore unknown outer and inner worlds, all these developments of the twentieth century have radically altered the human landscape of reality. If there was something noxious in these evolutions, that was, perhaps, not so much their novelty, but the speed with which they developed.

The particular views presented here must, therefore, be seen within this frame of "absolute relativity." A personal bias is admitted without apology, since it is epistemologically inescapable and of necessity qualifies, or infects the nature of any "reality."

The psychoanalytic bias holds that "reality" is first constructed in the mind – the psyche – even though this is a somatic mind, a "bodily mind" determined by the laws of genetics. Reality is first "conceived" there and then "found" in the world. We are constrained to having pre-conceptions and pre-conceptions of pre-conceptions along the road linking the two ends. Such a model of a two-tiered reality led, understandably, to the particular view of theater that is presented here, namely that of theater as a "repetition" of a former "primal" reality. The Aristotelian *mimesis* finds its ultimate meaning in this perspective. Accordingly, we have suggested that theater has its roots in a primal unconscious phantasy of the origin of the individual as the result of the rupture and division of a primordial psychosomatic One (motherinfant), a foundational event that was birth and death at the same time. The schism of the primal Unit gave rise to ontological duality which is, thus, considered as an *a priori* of human identity. The conflict within the *I* that was generated as the result of the division of the original Unit defines the tragic in human affairs. Theater in enacting the primal scene of the origin of the individual in a generative-deadly fissure of One-ness is fundamentally tragic. It is structured by loss and a continuous search for the "other reality" – a deep-rooted need to dialogue with what is lost. The *I*, now marked by a "lack," goes out looking for its ghost, the part that was, once, part of its own substance, the part that is now the *I-dead*, Death. Death is constitutive of the *I*. This explains our compulsive need for theater (in the multiple forms that theater takes). Theater stages the dis-union which is Death, the dis-junction that (de)structures the *I*. When the dis-junction and the destruction comes to be housed within the *I*, a "*whole I*" (living *and* dead) can make its appearance (subject to dis-appearance again).

The primal spectator: the infant looking at mother's face, the first mirror. This narcissistic image of the self, however, will soon change. Dis-illusion will follow as (m)other becomes Other, i.e., alien, separate, hostile: the visage of Death. This transformation, this dislocation from ipseity to alterity is traumatic to the budding ego. It is the *hamartia* – in the strictest Aristotelian sense – built into the psychobiological unit that compels it to endless repetitions of the primal traumatic scene: Theater. A process of healing?

Adopting such a perspective we found in Kantor's Theater of Death, a confirmation, but also an elucidation via emotion, as well as a penetrating subtle refinement of such views. We came to see his Theater of Death as an investigation into the very nature of theater, into theater's deeper nature. Kantor's focus on this, since the Return of Odysseus, was persistent, consistent and unwavering. The utterance "I am Odysseus" was not assuming a name, but, rather, the search for a name. And the search for theater's identity is *ipso facto* a search for human identity. To that end Kantor positioned himself at the site of the wound, "at the border" between two worlds: a Dionysian identity firmly planted on ambiguity. He became the "ford" in the river and invited us to join him there. This is the locus of the tragic which remains "open" and exposed to a double defeat. But the artist's choice is his action and, in this, Kantor masterfully indicates to us "the agonistic challenging animus of absolute tragedy."[1]

We attempted a formulation of the problem of theater that we considered to be the problem of the *I*. Kantor fought illusion. But any formulation is, essentially, a frame and, as such, it is the space of illusion. We are inseparable from our shadow as long as we exist. And, as long as we exist, "truth" can be granted to us only *in ludo*.

Konstantinos I. Arvanitakis
December 2016

Note

1 G. Steiner, *No Passion Spent* (New Haven: Yale U. P. 1996), 141.

References

Abraham, N. & M. Torok. *L'écorce et le noyau*. Paris: Flammarion, 1987.

Alford, C.F. *The Psychoanalytic Theory of Tragedy*. New Haven and London: Yale University Press, 1992.

Aristotle. *Nicomachean Ethics*. Translated by H. Rackham. Cambridge, MA: Harvard University Press, 1992.

Artaud, A. *Le théâtre et son double*. Paris: Gallimard, 1938.

Arvanitakis, K.I. "Dipl' ereo (A tale of doubles) The Bacchae." In *The Theban Cycle*, edited by C. Yiallouridis, 247–254. Athens: European Cultural Centre of Delphi, 2007.

Arvanitakis, K.I. "Nekromanteio Theatro." In *Kathodos*, edited by T. Terzopoulos, 280–287. Kiato: Katagramma, 2011.

Arvanitakis, K.I. *Psychoanalytic Scholia on the Homeric Epics*. Leiden: Brill, 2015.

Arvanitakis, K.I. "Some thoughts on the essence of the tragic." *Int. J. Psycho-Anal.*, 1998: 955–964.

Arvanitakis, K.I. "A theory of theater: theater as theory." *Psychoanal. Contemp. Thought*, 1998: 33–60.

Arvanitakis, K.I. "An update on time." *Int. J. Psycho-Anal.*, 2005: 531–534.

Aulagnier, P. *La violence de l'interprétation*. Paris: PUF, 1975.

Bablet, D. *Le théâtre de Tadeusz Kantor*. CNRS, 2006. DVD vidéo.

Badiou, A. *Éloge du théâtre*. Paris: Flammarion, 2013.

Beckett, S. *Three Occasional Pieces*. London: Faber & Faber, 1982.

Bergman, I. *Lanterna Magica*. Paris: Gallimard, 1987.

Bion, W. *Second Thoughts*. London: Karnac, 1984.

Blanchot, M. *L'espace littéraire*. Paris: Gallimard, 1955.

Blau, H. *Blooded Thought*. New York: Performing Arts Journal Publications, 1982.

Blau, H. *The Eye of Prey*. Bloomington and Indianapolis: Indiana University Press, 1987.

Botella, C. & S. Botella. "Psychic Figurability and Unrepresented States." In *Unrepresented States and the Construction of Meaning*, edited by H. Levine, W. Reed & D. Scarfone, 95–121. London: Karnac, 2013.

Bremmer, J. *The Early Greek Concept of the Soul*. Princeton, NJ: Princeton University Press, 1983.

Brook, P. *The Empty Space*. New York: Touchstone, 1996.

Burkert, W. *Greek Religion*. Translated by J. Raffan. Cambridge, MA: Harvard University Press, 1985.

Burkert, W. "Greek tragedy and sacrificial ritual." *Greek Roman and Byzantine Studies*, 1966: 87–121.

Burkert, W. *Homo Necans*. Translated by P. Bing. Berkeley: University of California Press, 1983.

Butcher, S.H. *Aristotle's Theory of Poetry and Fine Art*. New York: Dover Publications, 1951.

Calderon, P. *Life Is a Dream*. Mineola, NY: Dover Publications, 2002.

Campbell, D.A., trans. *Greek Lyric*. Vol. 1. Cambridge, MA: Harvard University Press, 1990.

Chataubriand, F.R. *Mémoires d' outre-tombei*. Paris: Le livre de Poche, 2001.

Chervet, B. *Le meurtre fondateur*. Paris: PUF, 2015.

Chrobak, J., L. Stangret, & M. Świca. *Tadeusz Kantor Wędrówka*. Kraków: Cricoteka, 2000.

Craig, E.G. *On the Art of the Theater*. New York: Theater Art Books, 1956.

Decreus, F. *The Ritual Theater of Theodoros Terzopoulos*. New York: Routledge, 2018.

Edmonds, J.M., trans. *Greek Elegy and Iambus*. Vol. 2. Cambridge, MA: Harvard University Press, 1979.

Ellman, M. *Psychoanalytic Literary Criticism*. London: Longman, 1994.

Else, G.F. *The Origins and Early Forms of Tragedy*. Cambridge, MA: Harvard University Press, 1967.

Farro, A. "Transformations in dreams and characters in the psychoanalytic field." *Int. J. Psycho-Anal.*, 2009: 209–230.

Ferrari, P.F. & G. Rizzolatti. "Mirror neuron research: the past and the future." *Philos. Trans. Royal Soc. London B Biol. Sci.* 369, 1644, 2014: 20130169.

Fischer-Lichte, E. *Theater, Sacrifice, Ritual*. New York: Routledge, 2005.

Freud, S. *La naissance de la psychanalyse*. Translated by A. Berman. Paris: PUF, 1969.

Freud, S. *The Standard Edition of the Complete Psychological Works of Sigmund Freud*. Edited and translated by J. Strachey. London: Hogarth Press, 1981.

Girard, R. *La violence et le sacré*. Paris: Grasset, 1972.

Green, A. *Un oeil en trop*. Paris: Les Éditions de Minuit, 1969.

Grotowski, J. *Towards a Poor Theater*. New York: Simon and Schuster, 1968.

Halczak, A. *Teatr Cricot 2 Informator 1989–1990*. Kraków: Cricoteka, 1991.

Harrison, J.E. *Themis: A Study of the Social Origins of Greek Religion*. New York: University Books, 1962.

Hegel, G.F. *Aesthetics: Lectures on Fine Arts*. Translated by. T.M. Knox. Oxford: Clarendon Press, 1975.

Hegel, G.W.F. *The Phenomenology of Mind*. Translated by J.B. Baillie. New York: Harper and Row, 1967.

Heidegger, M. *Being and Time*. New York: Harper Collins, 1962.

Heidegger, M. *The Question of Being*. Translated by W. Kluback and J. Wilde. New York: Twayne, 1958.

Herodotus. *Historiae.* Translated by A.D. Godley. Cambridge, MA: Harvard University Press, 1981.

Hölderlin, F. "On Tragedy: 'Notes on Oedipus'." *Comparative Criticism*, 1983: 203.

Homer. *Homeri Opera.* Edited by D.B. Munro and T.W. Allen. Translated by the author. London: Oxford Classical Texts, 1920.

Homer. *The Odyssey.* Translated by A.T. Murray. Cambridge, MA: Harvard University Press, 1995.

Isaacs, S. "The Nature and Function of Phantasy." *Int. J. Psycho-Anal.*, 1948: 73–97.

Kantor, T. *The Dead Class, Director's Notebook.* Kraków: Cricoteka Archives, 1975.

Kantor, T. *The Dead Class, Première.* November 15, 1975. Program.

Kantor, T. *Entretiens.* Paris: Editions Carré, 1996.

Kantor, T. *Guide to the performance of Let the Artists Die.* Translated by the author. Kraków: Cricoteka, 1988.

Kantor, T. *A Journey Through Other Spaces.* Edited and translated by M. Kobialka. Berkeley: University of California Press, 1993.

Kantor, T. *Métamorphoses.* Translated by the author. Paris: Hachette, 1982.

Kantor, T. "The Theater of Death." *TDR*, 1975: 137–148.

Kantor, T. *Wielopole, Wielopole.* Translated by M. Tchorek & G.M. Hyde. London: Marion Boyars Publishers, 1990.

Kantor, T. *Wielopole, Wielopole.* Kraków: Drukarnia Narodowa, 1984. Program.

Kirk, G.S. *The Bacchae by Euripides.* Englewood Cliffs, NJ: Prentice-Hall, 1970.

Kirk, G.S. & J.E. Raven. *The Presocratic Philosophers.* Cambridge: Cambridge University Press, 1971.

Klein, M. *Envy and Gratitude & Other Works.* New York: Delta, 1977.

Klein, M. "The importance of symbol-formation in the development of the ego." *Int. J. Psycho-Anal.*, 1930: 24–39.

Klein, M. *Love, Guilt and Reparation & Other Works.* New York: Delta, 1977.

Kobialka, M., ed. and trans. *A Journey Through Other Spaces.* By T. Kantor. Berkeley: University of California Press, 1993.

Kobialka, M. "Wielopole, Wielopole, Partytura." In *Further On Nothing*, edited by M. Kobialka, 291. Minneapolis: University of Minnesota Press, 2009.

Kristeva, J. *Polylogue.* Paris: Seuil, 1977.

Kristeva, J. *Pouvoirs de l' horreur.* Paris: Seuil, 1980.

Lacan, J. *Écrits.* Paris: Seuil, 1966.

Lacoue-Labarthe, P. "Theatricum Analyticum." *Glyph*, 2, 1977: 136.

Laplanche, J. & J-B Pontalis. "Fantasme originaire, fantasmes des origins, origine du fanatasme." *Les Temps Modernes*, 1964: 1833–1868.

Laplanche, J. & J-B Pontalis. *Vocabulaire de la psychanalyse.* Paris: PUF, 1976.

Leclaire, S. *On tue un enfant.* Paris: Seuil, 1975.

Lehmann, H-T. *Postdramatic Theater.* Translated by K. Jürs-Munby. New York: Routledge, 2006.

Loewald, H. "Psychoanalysis as an art and the fantasy character of the psychoanalytic situation." *J. Amer. Psychoanal. Assn.*, 1975: 277–299.

Lorca, F.G. *Selected Poems*. Translated by. M. Sorrell. New York: Oxford University Press, 2007.

Lorenz, K. *On Aggression*. Toronto: Bantam, 1967.

Martinis, R. *Tadeusz Kantor – CRICOT 2*. Salerno/Milano: Oedipus edizioni, 2001.

McDougall, J. *Theaters of the Mind: Illusion and Truth on the Psychoanalytic Stage*. New York: Brunner-Routledge, 1991.

Müller, H. *Gasammelte Irrtümer*. Vol. 3. Berlin: Verlag der Autoren, 1996.

Müller, H. *Die Gedichte*. Vol. 1. Frankfurt am Main: Suhrkamp, 1998.

Müller, H. *GermaniaI*. New York: Semiotext(e), 1990.

Nietzsche, F. *The Birth of Tragedy from the Spirit of Music*. Translated by W. Kaufmann. New York: Random House, 1967.

Otto, R. 1995. *Le Sacré*. Paris: Payot, 1995.

Otto, W.F. *Dionysus, Mythos und Kultus*. Frankfurt: Vittorio Klostermann, 1933.

Perron, R. "The Unconscious and Primal Phantasies." *Int. J. Psycho-Anal.*, 2001: 583–595.

Pickard-Cambridge, A.W. *Dithyramb, Tragedy and Comedy*. Oxford: Oxford University Press, 1927.

Plato. *Platonis Opera*. Edited by J. Burnet. London: Oxford University Press, 1973.

Plato. *The Republic*. Translated by F.M. Cornford. Oxford: Oxford University Press, 1945.

Pleśniarowicz, K. *The Dead Memory Machine*. Translated by W. Brand. Aberystwyth: Black Mountain Press, 2004.

Rank, O. *The Trauma of Birth*. New York: Dover Publications, 1929.

Ridgeway, W. *The Origin of Tragedy*. New York: Benjamin Blom, 1966.

Rimbaud, A. *Oeuvres completes*. Paris: Pléiade, 2009.

Rohde, E. *Psyche*. Translated by H.B. Willis. London, 1895.

Romanska, M. *The Post-traumatic Theater of Grotowski and Kantor*. London: Anthem Press, 2012.

Rozik, E. *The Roots of Theatre*. Iowa City: University of Iowa Press, 2002.

Schechner, R. *The Future of Ritual*. New York: Routledge, 2003.

Schechner, R. *Performance Theory*. New York: Routledge, 1988.

Scheler, M. "On the Tragic." *Cross Currents*, 1954: 178–191.

Schulz, B. *Les boutiques de cannelle*. Paris: Denoël, 1974.

Segal, C. *Dionysiac Poetics and Euripides' 'Bacchae'*. Princeton, NJ: Princeton University Press, 1982.

Segal, H. *Dream, Phantasy and Art*. New York: Routledge, 1991.

Segal, H. "Notes on Symbol Formation." *Int. J. Psycho-Anal.*, 1957: 135–141.

Snell, B. *Die Ausdrücke Für der Begriff des Wissens in der Vorplatonischen Philosophie*. Berlin: Weidmann, 1924.

Snell, B. *The Discovery of the Mind*. New York: Dover Publications, 1982.

Sophocles. *Antigone*. Translated by F. Storr. Cambridge, MA: Harvard University Press, 1981.

Steiner, G. *The Death of Tragedy*. New Haven: Yale University Press, 1961.

Steiner, G. *No Passion Spent*. New Haven: Yale University Press, 1996.

Storm, M. *After Dionysus*. Ithaka: Cornell University Press, 1998.

Turri, M.G. *Acting, Spectating and the Unconscious: A Psychoanalytic Perspective On Unconscious Processes of Identification in the Theater*. New York: Routledge, 2017.

von Wilamowitz-Moellendorff, U. *Der Glaube der Hellenen*. Berlin: Weidmann, 1931.

Way, A.S. *Euripides*. Cambridge, MA: Harvard University Press, 1979.

Winnicott, D.W. "Fear of Breakdown." *Int. Rev. Psycho-Anal.*, 1974: 103.

Winnicott, D.W. *Playing and Reality*. London: Tavistock Publications, 1971.

Winnicott, D.W. *Through Paediatrics to Psychoanalysis*. London: Hogarth, 1975.

Wright, E. "Psychoanalysis and the Theatrical: Analyzing Performance." In *Analysing Performance*, edited by P. Campbell, 175–190. Manchester: Manchester University Press, 1996.

Žižek, S. *The Parallax View*. Cambridge, MA: MIT Press, 2006.

Index

For Product Safety Concerns and Information please contact our EU representative GPSR@taylorandfrancis.com Taylor & Francis Verlag GmbH, Kaufingerstraße 24, 80331 München, Germany

Batch number: 08153762

Printed by Printforce, the Netherlands